EVEN GOD GETS DISTRACTED SOMETIMES

Luigi Coppola – www.LinkTr.ee/LuigiCoppola – poetry, music, rum and coke: Southbank Centre's New Poets Collective 23/24, Poetry Archive Worldview winner, Bridport Prize shortlist, Ledbury & National Poetry Competition longlist, produces music as 'The Only Emperor'

Mark Shuttleworth in the brambles in the bushes.

Luigi:
For Keeley, Isabella and Eliana.

Mark:
For me girls.

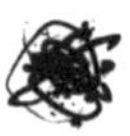

ISBN: 978-1-917617-17-8

Cover designed by Aaron Kent & Mark Shuttleworth

Edited and Typeset by Aaron Kent

Broken Sleep Books Ltd
PO BOX 102
Llandysul
SA44 9BG

CONTENTS

Even God Gets Distracted Sometimes

Poetry by Luigi Coppola
&
Art by Mark Shuttleworth

Broken Sleep Books

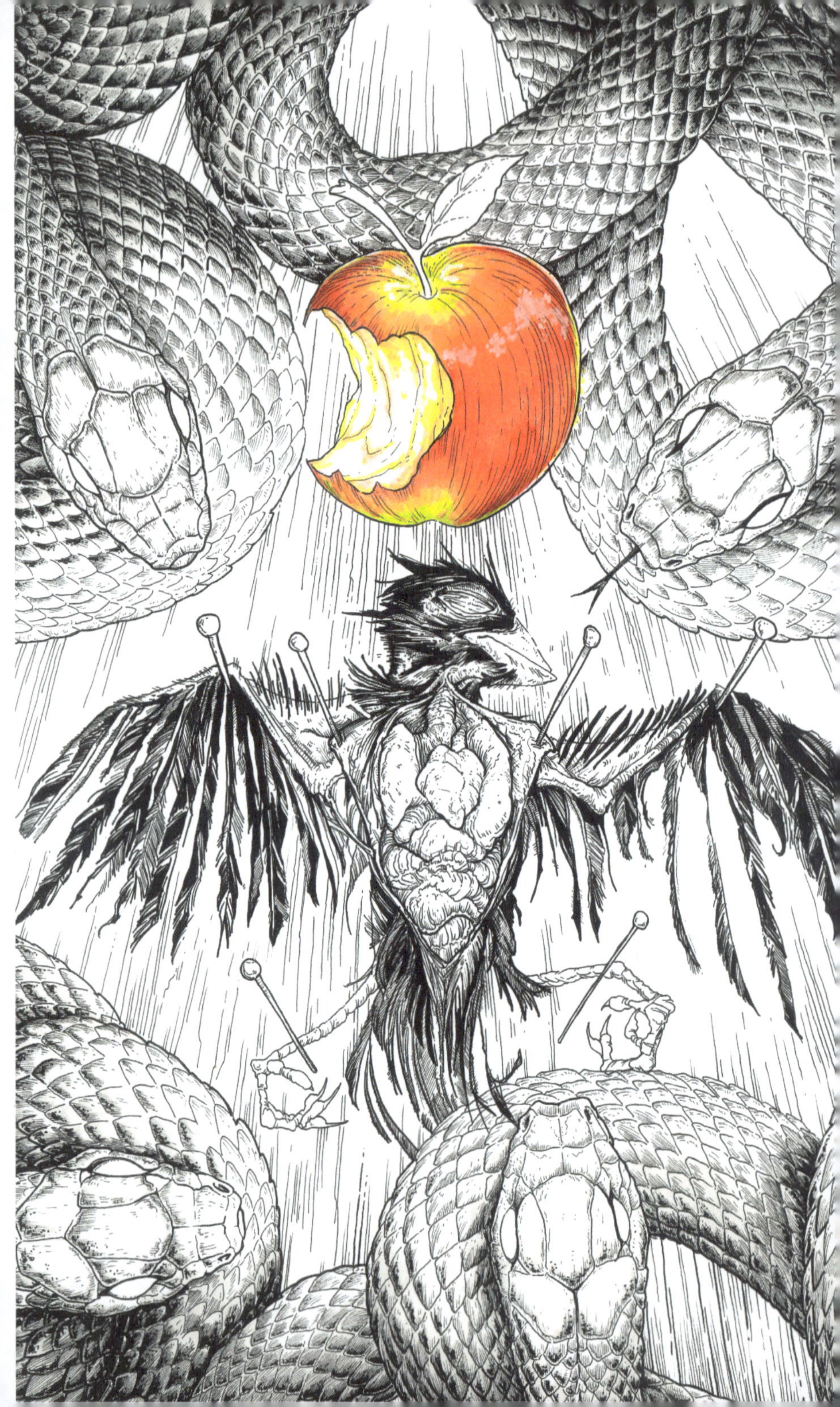

EVEN GOD GETS DISTRACTED SOMETIMES

I got halfway through then gave up:
the beak an empty orbit;
the breast strung out like a Stradivarius;
the wings thin as slices of rump veal
soaked in milky confidence.

I was thinking of tinkering with the tendons:
the first incarnation tore in half on take-off,
a failed soarless game – squalling
and screeching, ripping at its own guts
until they dissolved to pink bubbles.

The second one (mishmashed from matter
left over from that miscarriage of a brother)
did no better: it dived headfirst into a mountain,
collapsed during collision, waiting
to be reassembled. I recycled instead
for this third half-attempt and if
I had more time I would finish it.
Really, I would.

But now the wind stands still, the sun
sinks its shape into a lunar self, the light
echoes through my canvas corridor
as I hear last week's work whine.

Damn all those distractions to earth:
that serpent slithering, whispering again
and those two giggling malcontents
munching on something
they were told
explicitly
not to pluck.

www.linktr.ee/EvenGod

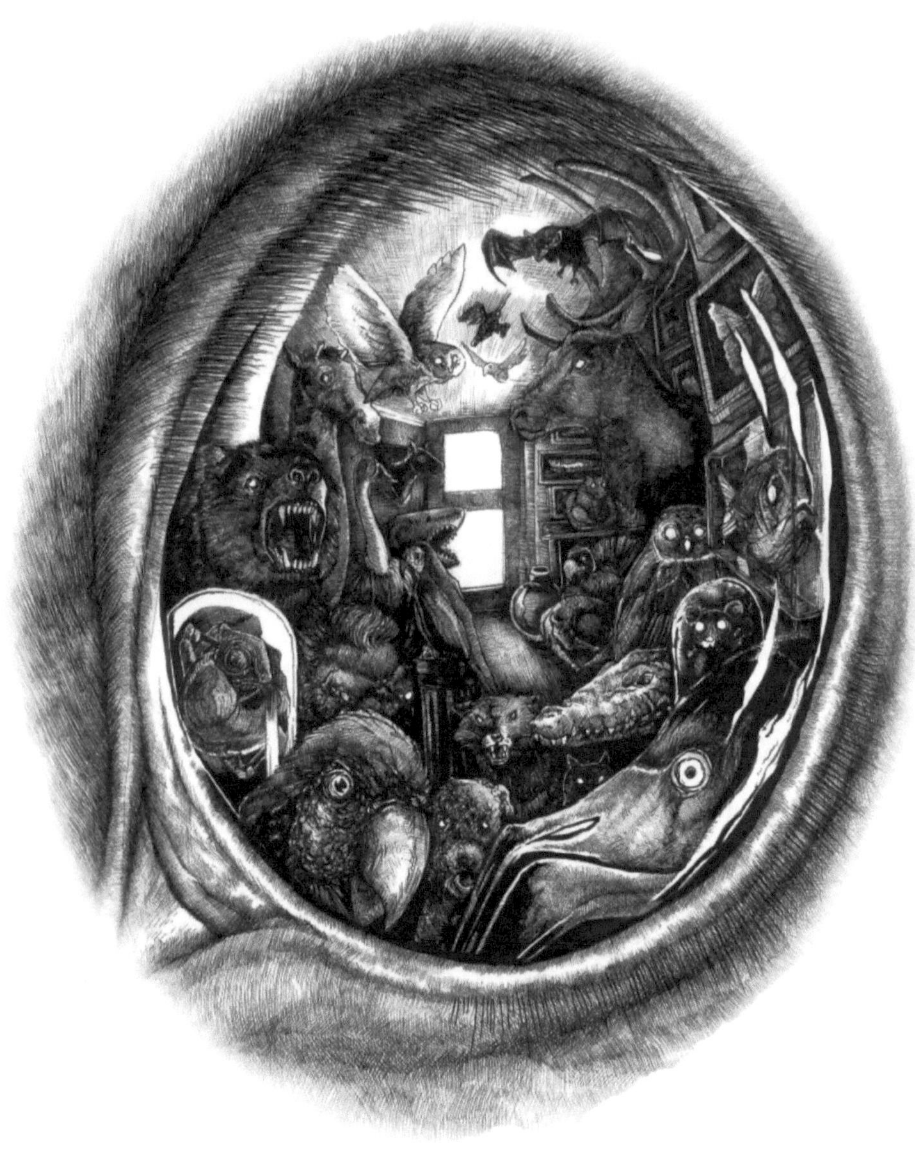

THE EYES OF ANIMALS

I'm looking through the shop window
at the filled rows, glass boxes and walls.
Did I mention the smell? Was there one?
Yes: it was musk, warmth, dust, alcohol
infusing this high street zoo of frozen frames.
Trim and pimped on quiet pedestals –
from open field, wood, stream to shelved
herd, flock, shoal of distant cousins.

I'm staring at the cow head: its pert ears
pointless satellites; its nose a dried oyster
glued back on slightly off-angle; its eyes,
in their wide blackness reflecting every blade,
fence, muddied machine and that final
hollowing out by prod then pistol.

www.linktr.ee/TheEyesOfAnimals

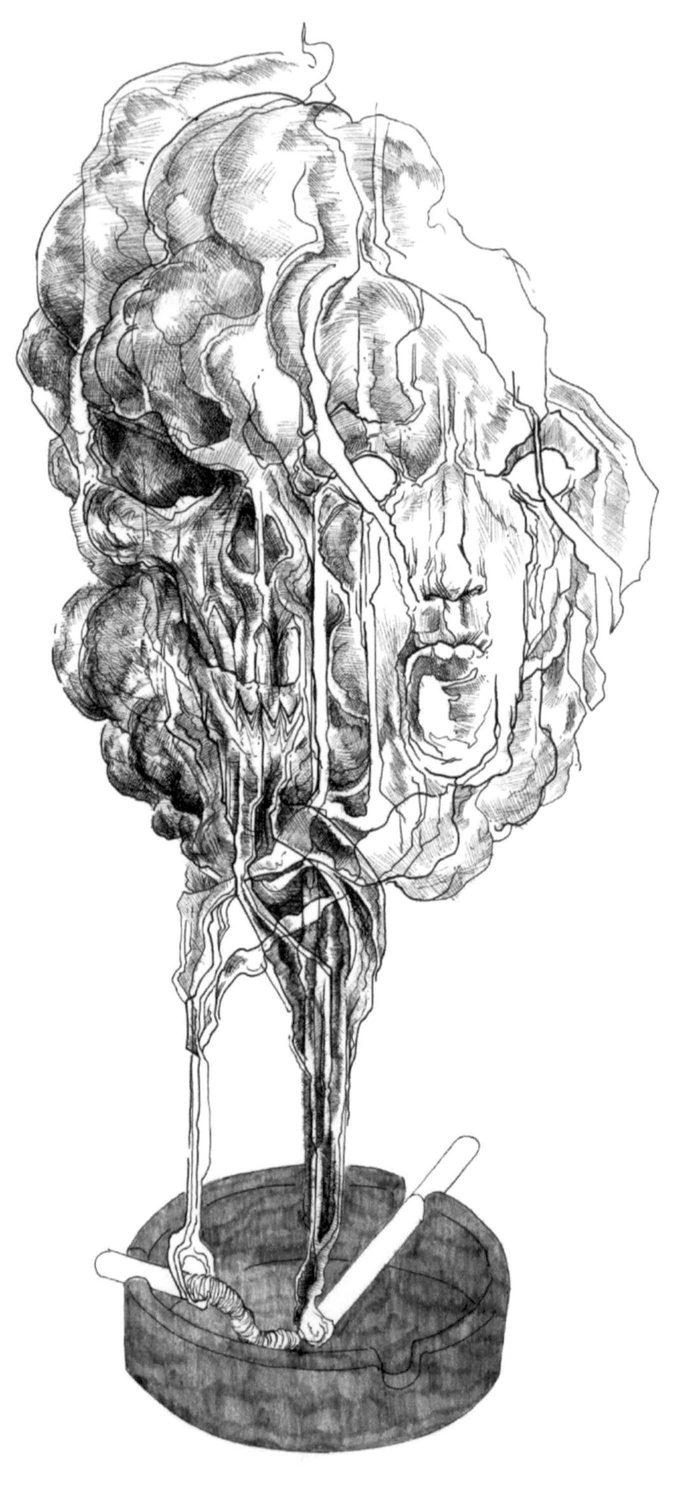

RENDEZVOUS

This is not happening
You are in a dream
A secret scene inside
The mirror's blinded eye

You don't feel this
Less than a paper cut
So thin and so fine
A tiny pinprick

You won't remember it
Here is your bag
And here is your coat
And there is the door

www.linktr.ee/RendezvousPoem

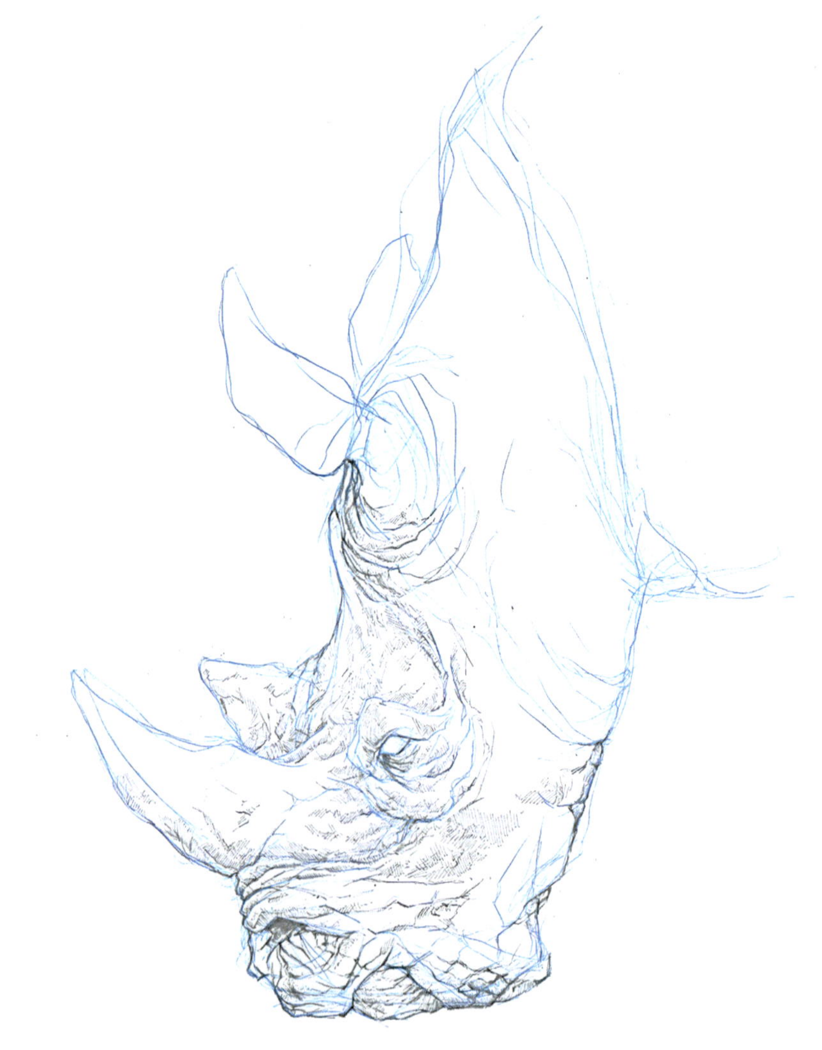

THE LAST WHITE RHINO FLIPS THE BIRD

and I don't mean oxpeckers pecking on my back;
those comrades squawk when danger appears
in its hats, with its guns, in wheeled juggernauts
not camouflaged enough for my tastes.

No, this is to you from nose-horn, from Black and White,
of Indian and of Javan and of Sumatran, though really all
of us are, erm, a greyish-brown: the colour of moist earth
and foreboding sky and whatever we find to eat.

This is from the tonne-plus behemoth, the mmwonker,
from one that bows to only elephants and extinction,
dangerous and endangered: stroke my armour, pray
at my bulk and, if you dare, kiss my horn.

We were the crash, the wijd, the horned-nose herd, amalgamation
of language and form across eons, browsing with soft muzzle,
prehensile and knowing, grazing for leaves, twigs and truth
amongst the shrinking plains and stripped bark.

Sure, our brothers and sisters – the horse, the zebra, the tapir,
the ass – have the same toes and tails, but who has the girth,
the weight, the mistake of size in a world too small, too loud,
too lustful for our bone, to saw and grind and sell.

Imagine every clipping from every finger and toenail
you have ever let fly across a room. Imagine every strand
of hair cut and allowed to be swept away. Imagine all that
diamond-compressed, sculpted in war, pointed to perfection

and then you would have me. But you have me already,
don't you? Across the cracked field, down the parched river,
past the split rocks, off my continent to a world of dead grey,
shining plates and forged weapons – too much for

my perfect grey, my pulsing plates, my proud weapon.
I can hear and smell your terror but am blind to your wrath.
Leave me to run on open land, to rub against arching trees,
to wallow in luxurious mud so it cakes across my bulk.

And leave me to dream, alone, of breeding one calf at a time
while three-year olds jostle in the herd's warmth. We were clear
– towering dung marks our land. So be careful where you stand
for every one of your footsteps are taken in our footprints,
now footnotes to the Anthropocene epoch.

www.linktr.ee/TheLastWhiteRhinoFlipsTheBird

WILD WHITE FACE

after 'Red Right Hand' by Nick Cave and the Bad Seeds

Down by the river where the trees all bow
They've pitched a funfair there
Where the rusted gates foreshadow the fate
Of a hare in a snare
Where the skelter climbs a thousand times
In the tolling chimes
Oh kid you thought
You'd handle all of those scares
Round the twister, swung by swinger
Down the skyfall, up the stairs
Stamping tickets at the stall
Is a suited disgrace
A smile cracked open
On his Wild White Face

He'll show you all the sights
Whisper secrets, all his hints and tips
He'll guide you through the crowd
Pick you up when you fall down
Or are tripped
He'll take you off to the side
Rearrange your insides
And all you'll do is scream and holler
That you want more
He's a corpse, he's ghoul
He's a seer, he's a mystic
They're scrawling his name
All over this place
His eyeballs rolling
In his Wild White Face

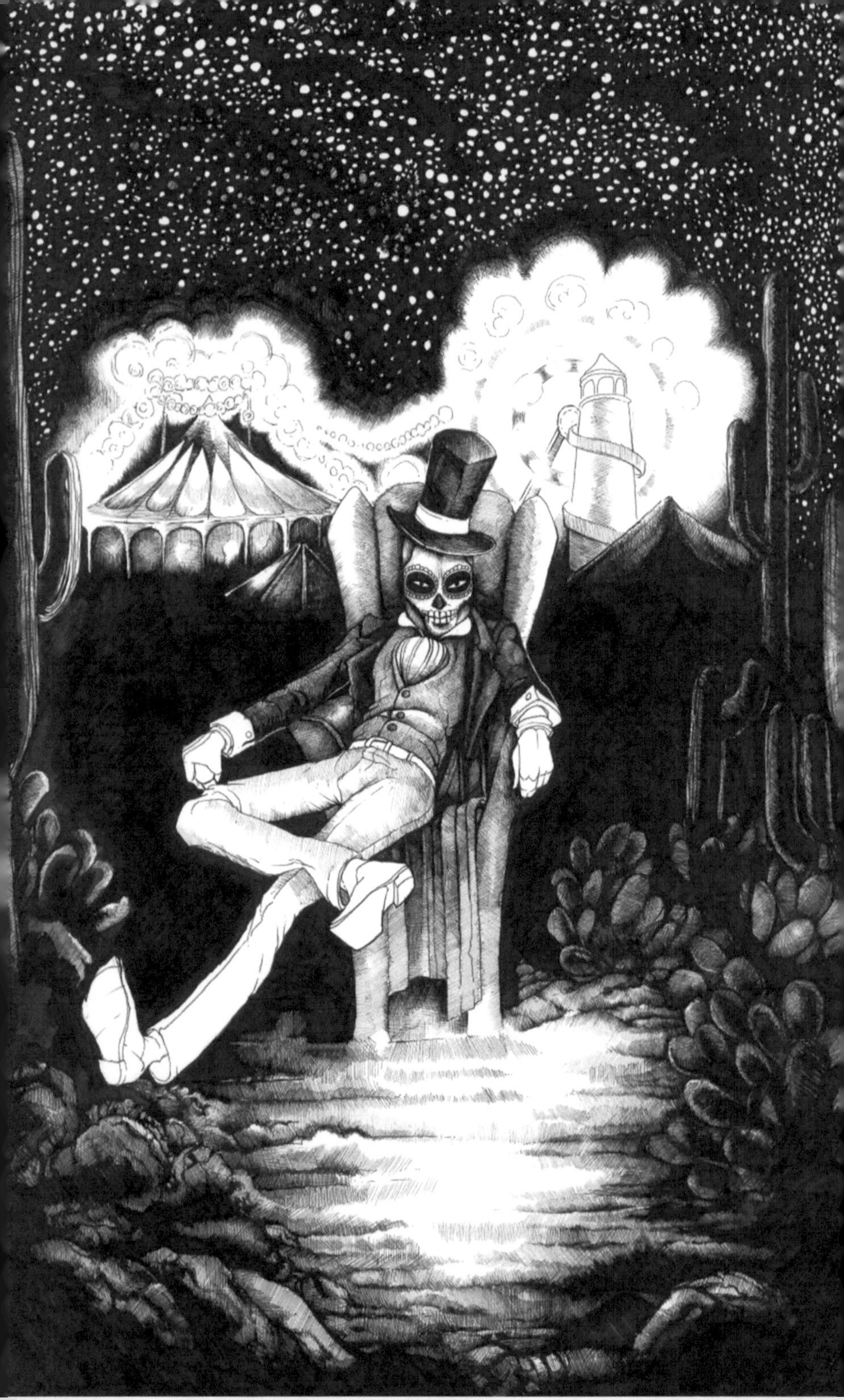

You think they start too high
He'll help you up
You think they go too fast
He's got teacups
You feel like you gonna be sick
You feel like you've been kicked
Ah kid, you know
He's got you something to sup
Here's some candy, here's some apple
Here's some whiskey for your cup
His reflection seems to warp
All of time and space
As a cackle echoes out
From his Wild White Face

You'll find him next year on this field
But sooner than that
In the shadow in the corner of your room
In the purr of a black cat
You'll find him under the sheets
In the wireless' hum
Hey kid, I'm telling you
Please, don't turn it up
He's a corpse, he's ghoul
He's a seer, he's a mystic
We're just embryotic rats
In his diabolic race
Announced and narrated
By his Wild White Face

www.linktr.ee/WildWhiteFace

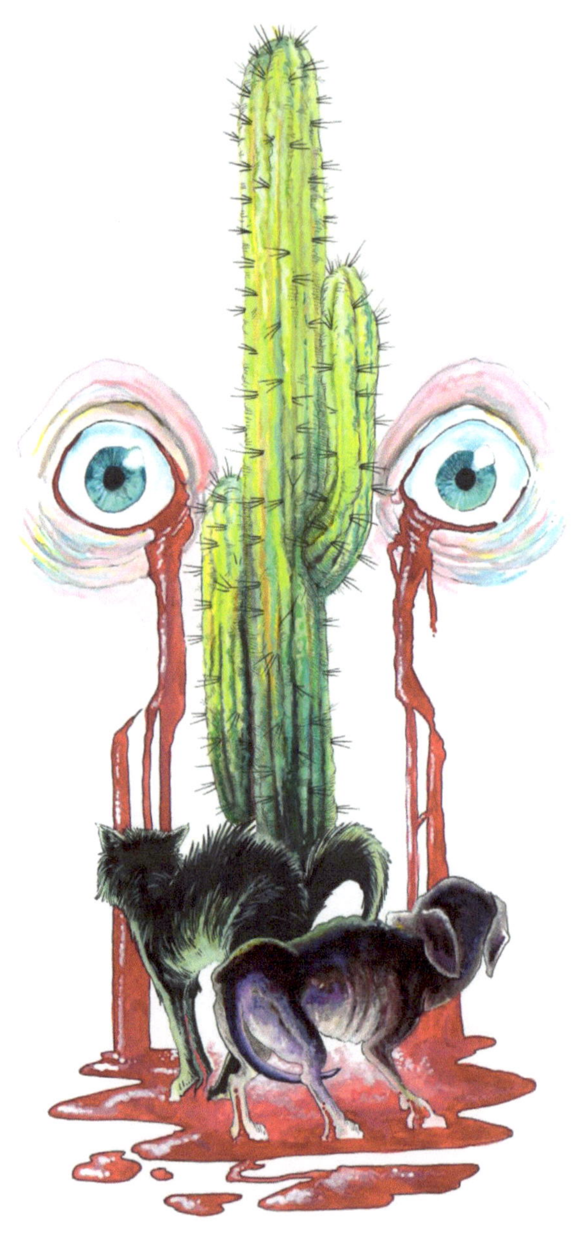

CACTUS

Cats ran away; dogs howled
until freed, never fed;
goldfish played dead until dead;
even stones cracked
themselves – better to split
than stay put.

It wasn't until a cactus,
bought at a closing-down sale,
that something other than animal,
mineral, shadow or silhouette
lived in those four walls and
gave as good as it didn't get.

By midnight, he hugged
it to sleep: spikes rested
in him, green skin against
blooded, clasped palms.

www.linktr.ee/CactusPoem

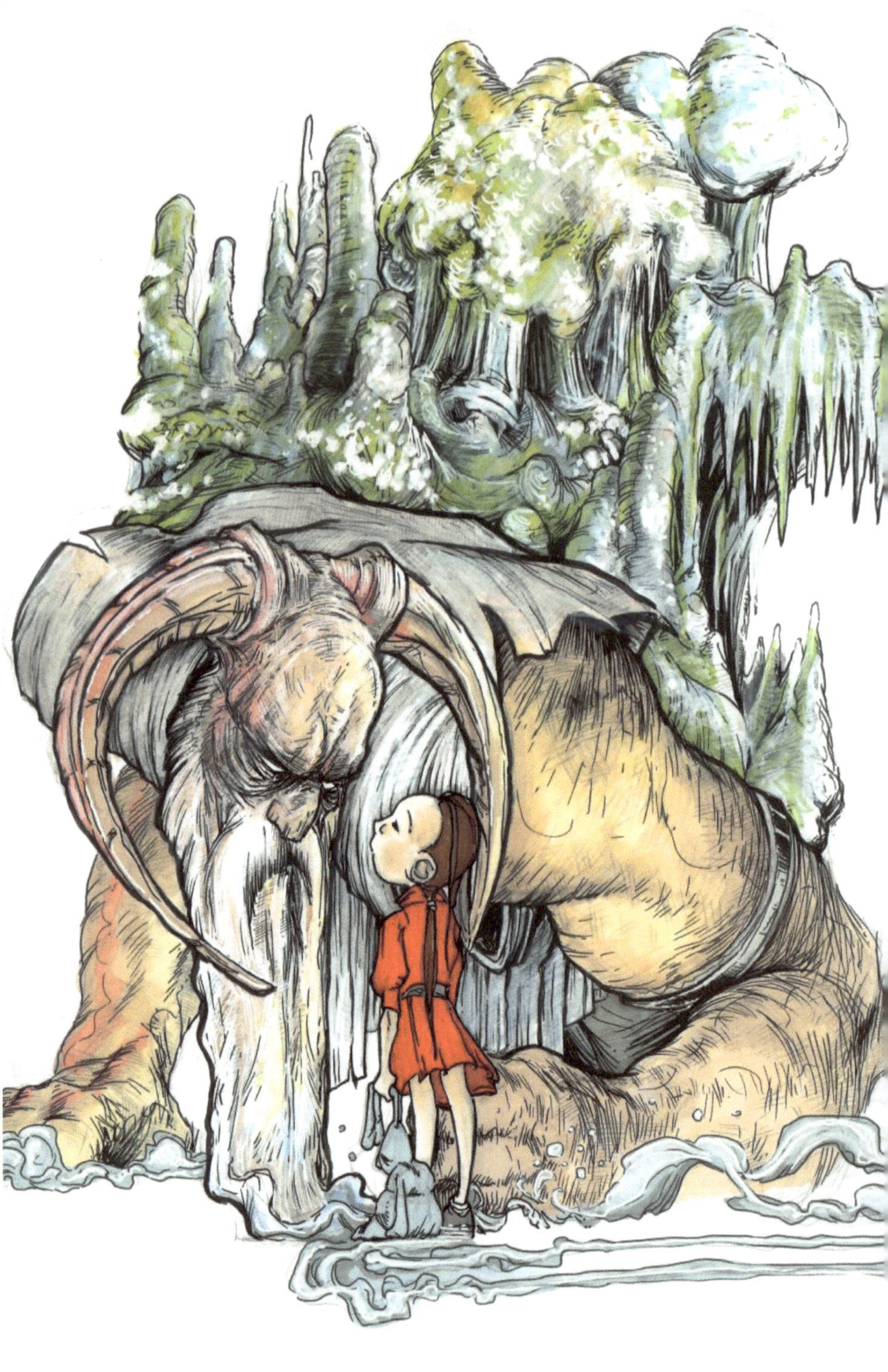

WHAT OLD FATHER EARTH ASKED OF HIS DAUGHTER

Come my daughter, come and play
No my father, I cannot stay
But I have built a world for you
I am sorry father, it will not do
What if I told you about the trees
That sing and dance with the laughing breeze
I am sorry father, they will not please
What if I told you about the cave
Where imps and sprites all rush and rave
I am sorry father, I do not crave
What if I told you about the stream
Where golden fish all strobe and beam
I am sorry father, I am not keen
Then tell me child, what do you need?
What can I make to keep you a seed?
I am sorry father, I need the sky
Where my mother is free to fly
I need the sea where sisters drift
I need the dew where aunties lift
I need the mist that grandmothers sift
It is not you, you are not to blame
But father and daughter are not the same
You build on earth, you call it home
My kin and I must rove and roam
Then I will rumble and I will quake
I will destroy and I will unmake
I will cave in and I will tear down
I will burn and I will drown
Unless oh child, oh daughter you stay
Oh no my father, not even a single day

www.linktr.ee/WhatOldFatherEarthAsked

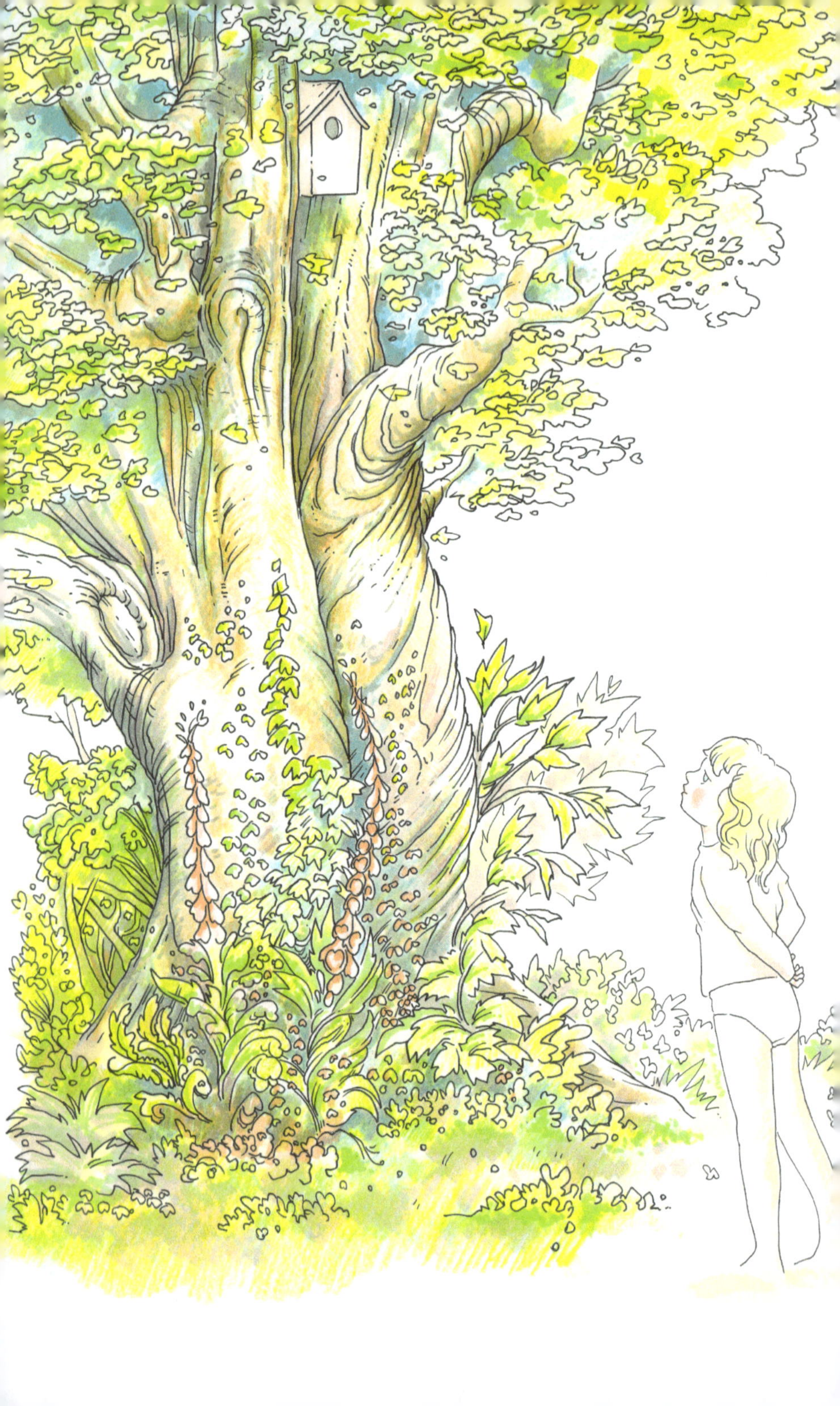

AUTUMN WAITING

Our family's land once rolled all the way
to the horizon. We had pitched in with our pitch:
digging ditches and tracing furrows across sun-
soaked land that yielded all we had needed.

And we worshipped the visiting animals:
the foxes and their searching eyes;
the badgers and their rooting noses;
the rats and their scurrying habits.

But the birds held a special place.
We left seed on walls and watched them dive
then hop along the top, pecking at crumbling brick,
their slight frames shimmering against the red.

We would gather twigs and leaves, offerings
left at the bottom of the garden at the base of the oak,
old and knotted and twisted through years and minds
after our father's father's father had planted it.

Now our father had made a different gift –
with timber shorn and salvaged from the storm-
wrecked shed – a tiny gabled-roofed, portholed home,
lined with our sheep's wool, picked for the fence.

And with Autumn waiting, we watched

www.linktr.ee/AutumnWaiting

his hands smooth the sides, round the edges,
screw it all together, firm and steady –
he had learnt his lesson from the shed debacle.

I loved the brush strokes. He stained the outside
with a thick water – a blessing that brought out the grain,
the dark rings of years straightened to lines along a man-
made plane, its fumes stinging noses and weeping eyes.

The morning was ending while he stood teetering
on ladder. As he stretched, grunts timed with hammer
blows, oak solid against his thundering hand
with the perfect alcove prised open by her hand

perfectly sized for this new home. It was as if she knew that,
decades later, we would be here, then, filling that gap
for a life to fly in and nest in and lay in and to warm
and to hatch and to feed and to leave.

As we did. Decades again after that, I stood in the same
spot, old yolk replacing a mere egg, the oak bowed,
the field brown, the house empty – but the birdbox still there,
echoing a new age's call, with my mind
echoing inside its walls.

THE DEATH OF A DEEP SEA DIVER

Hydrostatically-induced barotrauma is
the worst: blood boiling without heat,
eyes bulging without release, mind spinning
while sinking – stationary, weighted, waiting.

The lure of cue-ball pearls with seaweed strings,
sleeping sovereigns in water-warped chests,
shipwrecks in a sifted grave –
these are the things I crave.

And this slow-motion crash scene
of buckled metal and emerald flakes,
of soiled timber and unravelled rope
floating away like snakeskin
is what I find myself in –
or rather where it finds me.

And it is a sickness: the blood boiling withou–
wait, I told you that already, didn't I?
Did I mention the eyes? Er...

What about the lungs? No?
They are balloon scraps, stretched
and French-kissed back to a brittle buoyance.

My ears appear to be blocked
as if a trident thrusted through

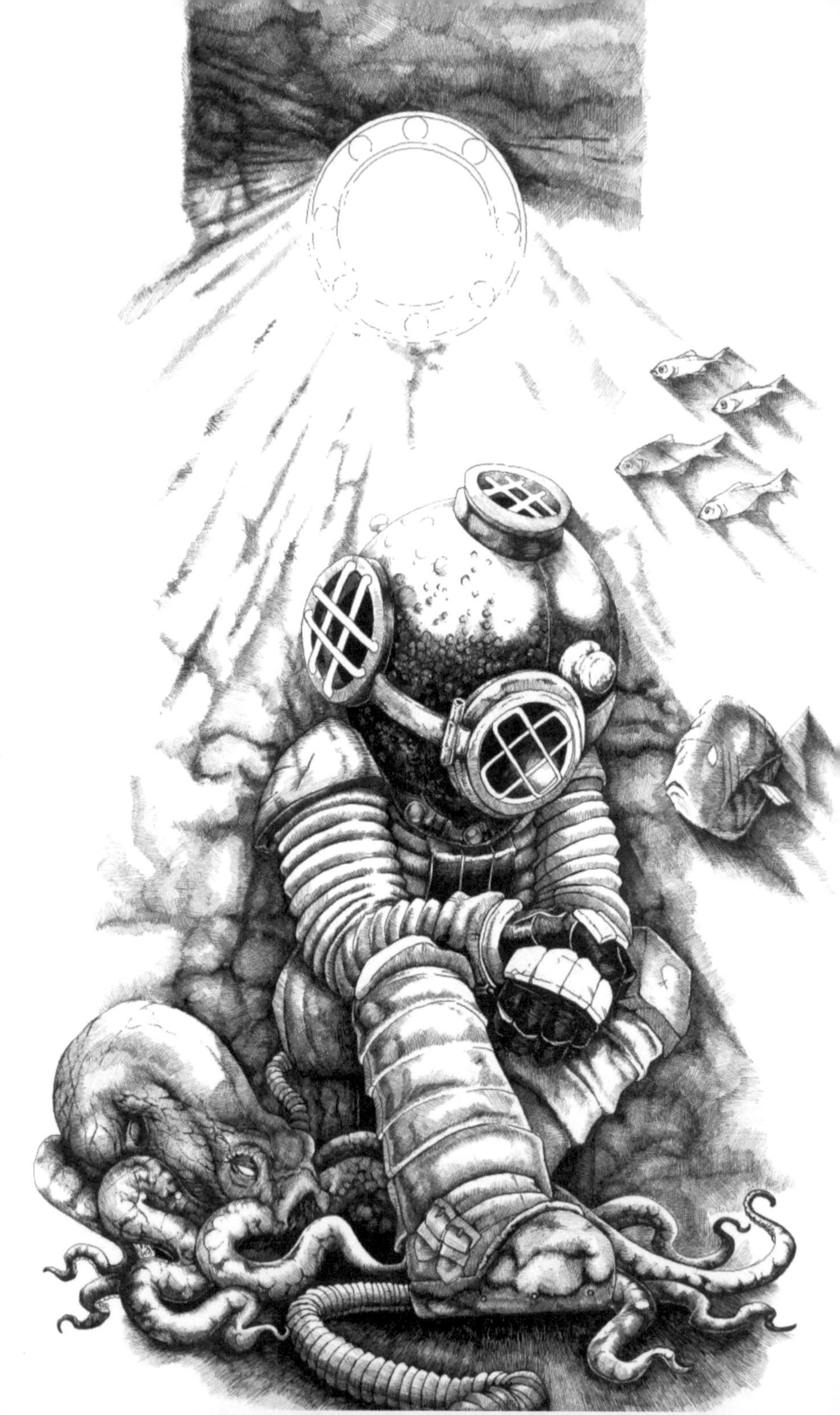

and threaded one end with the other.
My teeth fracture and fray, a salted decay:
I grind and let the chalk froth up.

But at least I have company:
Fred and his friends bubble
their secret *Oh*s and *Ah*s;
Olly arms wrestles and always seems to win;
Sharon noses the porthole – she pretends
to wink with her two black eyes
and hides a smile
through a thousand teeth.

But from this wrought reef,
I miss the sun,
I miss the sand, any land
that doesn't sink
with every step, somewhere firm
and dry and safe –
a mile away as the dolphin swims,
an eon of selection
as the human evolves.

So I step on the cable,
take a last breath and
wait.

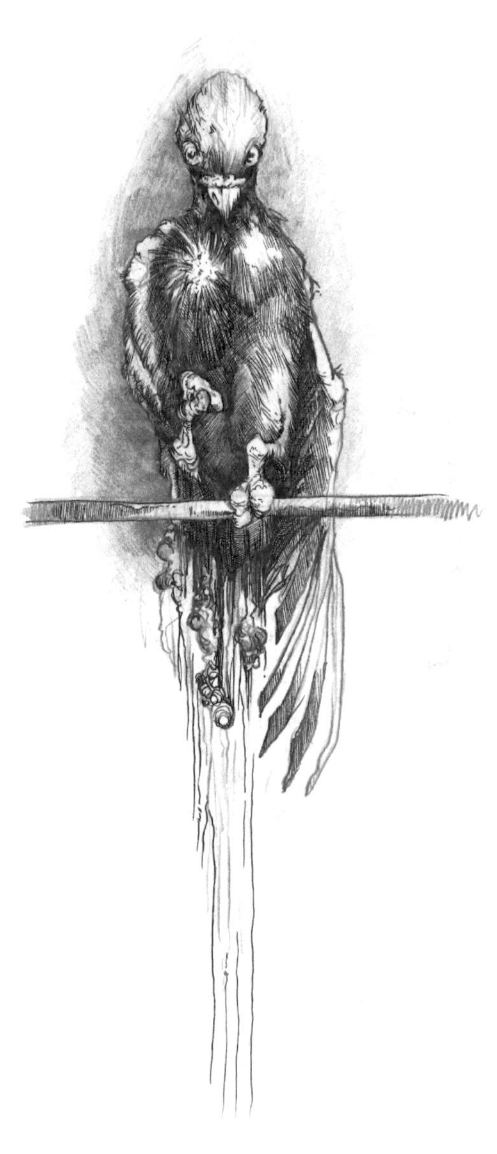

THE PIGEON

after 'The Eagle' by Alfred Lord Tennyson

He claws the curb with crannied digits;
Near to a bin he pecks and fidgets,
Wrung with salmonella, rickets.

Between the frothing cars he dashes;
He flops with fractured wings and thrashes,
And like a stumbling drunk he crashes.

www.linktr.ee/ThePigeonAfterTennyson

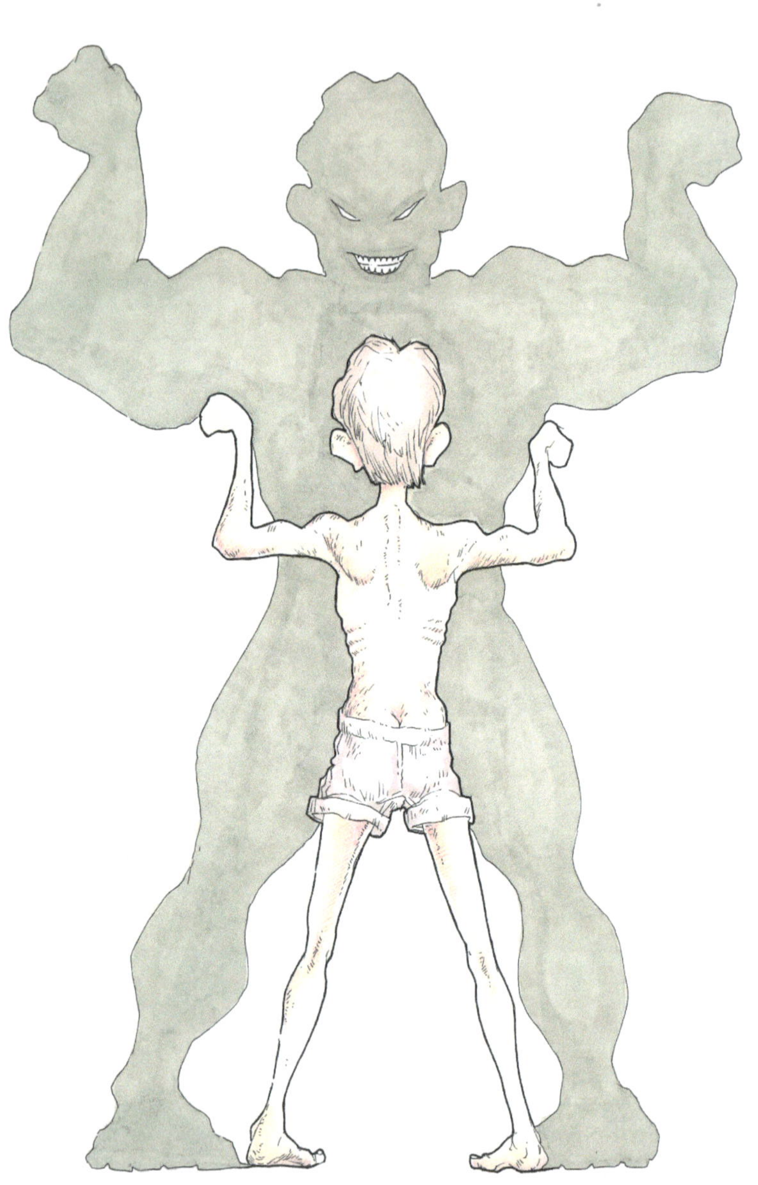

MY SHADOW

I saw it

Don’t tell me I didn’t

It moved without
Beyond me

I thought I dreamt it
Flexing and pirouetting
But it was just being ironic

So I slowly stepped out of its feet
Stumbled
Ran away

Only time has ever caught up that quickly

I panicked and raised my hand
Scratching my head to think
Just as it hit me
Right on the temple

I boxed and kickboxed
But it met each limb with its own
And socked me one

I fell on my back
With it sliding under me
Whispering

See ya next time

The sun will blind me first

www.linktr.ee/MyShadowPoem

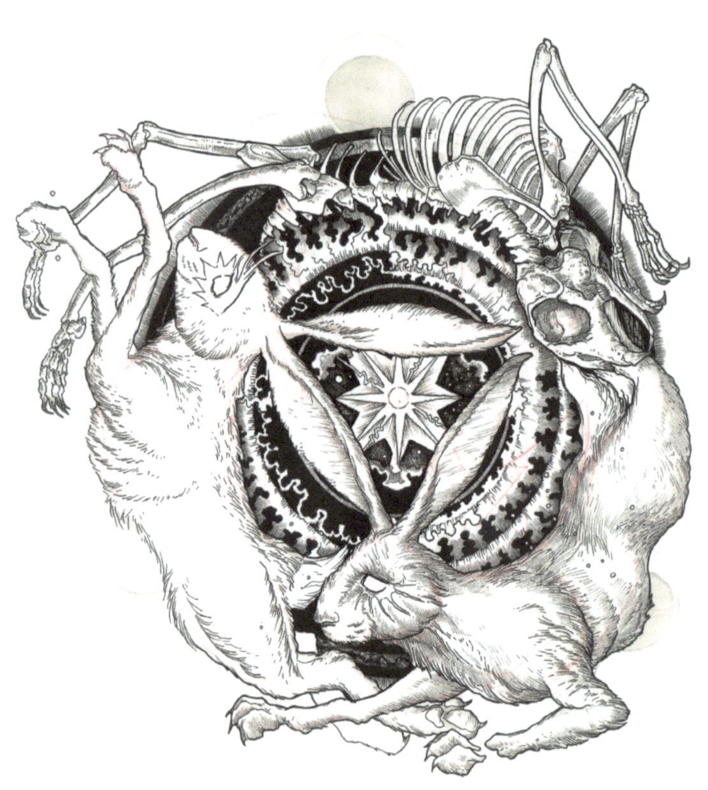

HARES AND RABBITS

The rabbits' rapid racing hides
the fearful, nervous hearts inside.
Hares' ears twitch when howls are heard
and off they go so furred and spurred.

Oh Ēostre! Oh Artemis!
Watch over blood-shot eyes.
Oh Holda! Oh Aphrodite!
Hear their chattering cries.

Across the field and into burrow,
hares know danger in their marrow.
Kittens of rabbits clamour to a warmth
as dirt shakes down from crumbling walls.

Oh El-ahrairah! Oh Tu-er Shen!
Oh Wenenut! Oh protect them!
Keep them from harm, from any threat –
never let their skinned sun set.

www.linktr.ee/HaresAndRabbits

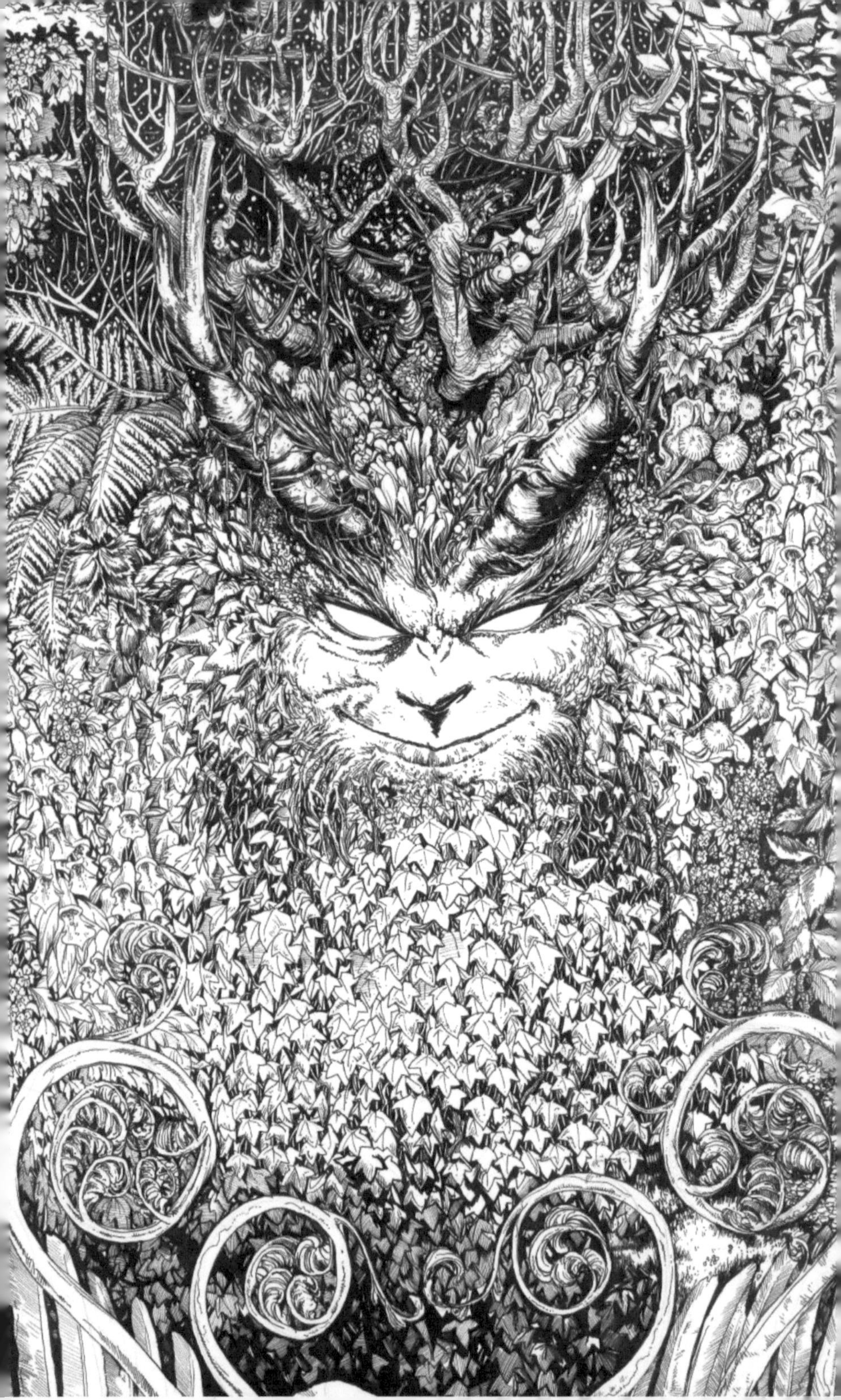

VILLANELLE FOR THE GREENMAN

Where nature's visage shows the sheen of sun
And life grows as seared soil meets vivid sky
The Greenman lives and all will live as one

We witness first when cold death's course has run
Through rotting remnants left where beasts fall, die
Then nature's mouth can sup on sleeping sun

Watch earth reclaim that far-gone flesh for fun
Devour riches found when end comes nigh
When Greenman eats, we all shall feast as one

The patient, budding, feeding force won't shun
Nor waste a single scrap – we can't deny
That nature's hand will share that salvaged sun

For green will grow from grey and brown and dun
And green will spread to leaf and tree and rye
As Greenman blooms so all shall grow as one

Yes, all old life will blossom bright and none
Can break the bond that births and lifts us high
With nature's heart we'll grace the gift of sun
When Greenman comes and all can love as one

www.linktr.ee/VillanelleForTheGreenman

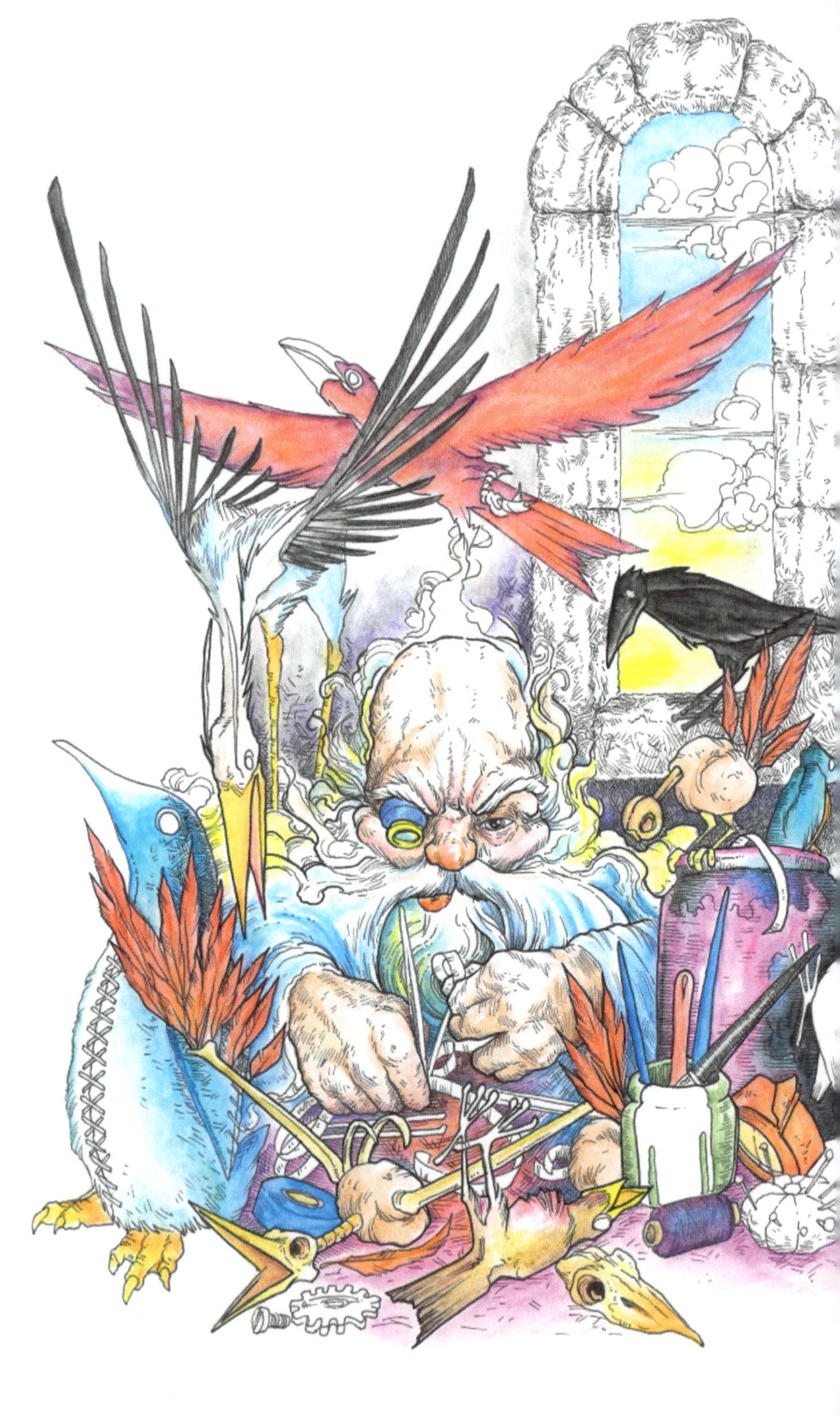

THE RAVEN'S BORN

He clasps the glistening clay inside his hand
and kneads and works and shapes and smooths and bakes
while hordes of sculpted birds awkwardly stand
and screech and squawk – some mere trials or mistakes:
the magpie snatched a ring and skulked away;
the dove smirked, snapped the branch within its beak;
the owl twitchingly stared in shock, dismay;
the phoenix detonated with a shriek;
the mockingbird sang one sole song (so lazy);
the pigeon struck the stone wall with a thwack;
the peacock got cocky; the cuckoo, crazy;
the crow chased worms and then never came back.
But the raven stands still, poised every dawn,
and that was how this bird's legend was born.

www.linktr.ee/TheRavensBorn

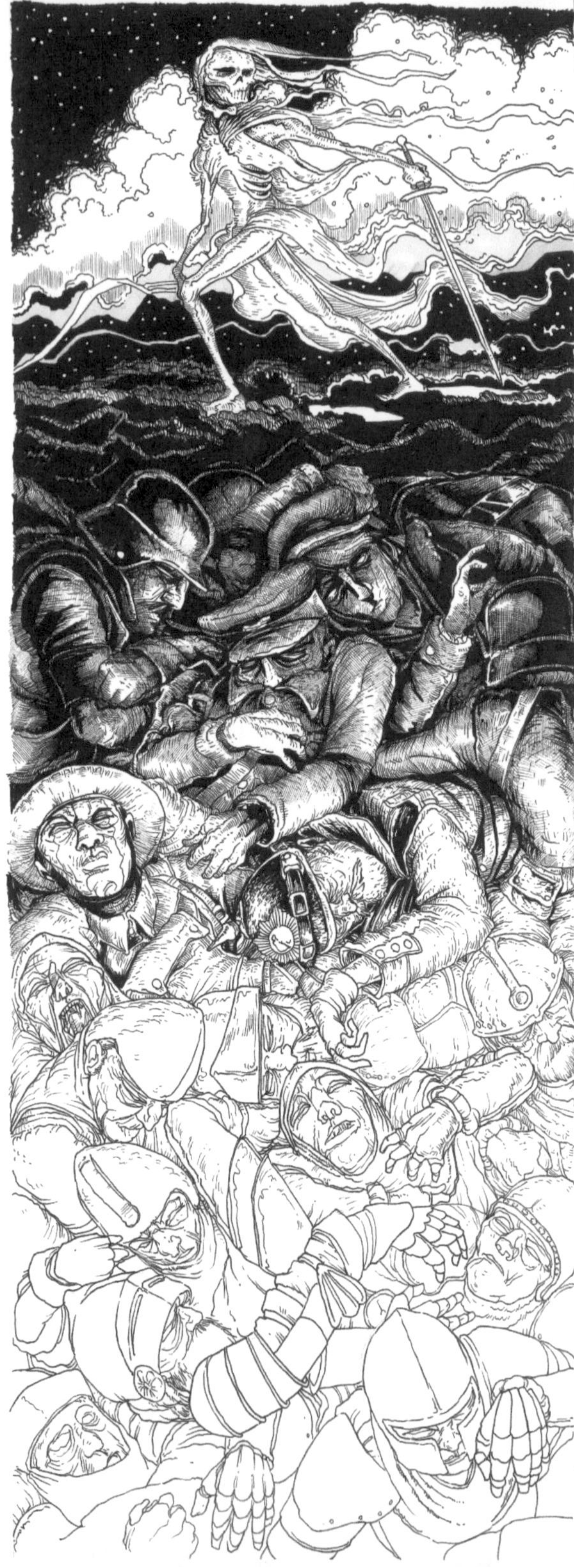

DEATH WRITES AN OPEN LETTER

I have set my scythe down
for only the third time in eternity:
the first was at 11am on the eleventh day
of the eleventh month;

the second was at midnight as Attlee
spoke of last enemies laid low,
though he and I would come to know
the end of that fight was only respite.

This third time, today, now,
this very moment you read these words
that I have wanted to write so
many times before to let you know:
you have filled my home

with too many of your own.
And be sure that this pause,
where pen and paper
replace gun and sword,
is not for long
for I will do my duty
as you will do yours.

Then when we meet
and you have lived a life
and sought for right
and fought the good fight
and did all you said you would,
I hope you are old and wise and grey
not young and green and red.

Yours faithlessly,

Death

www.linktr.ee/DeathWritesAnOpenLetter

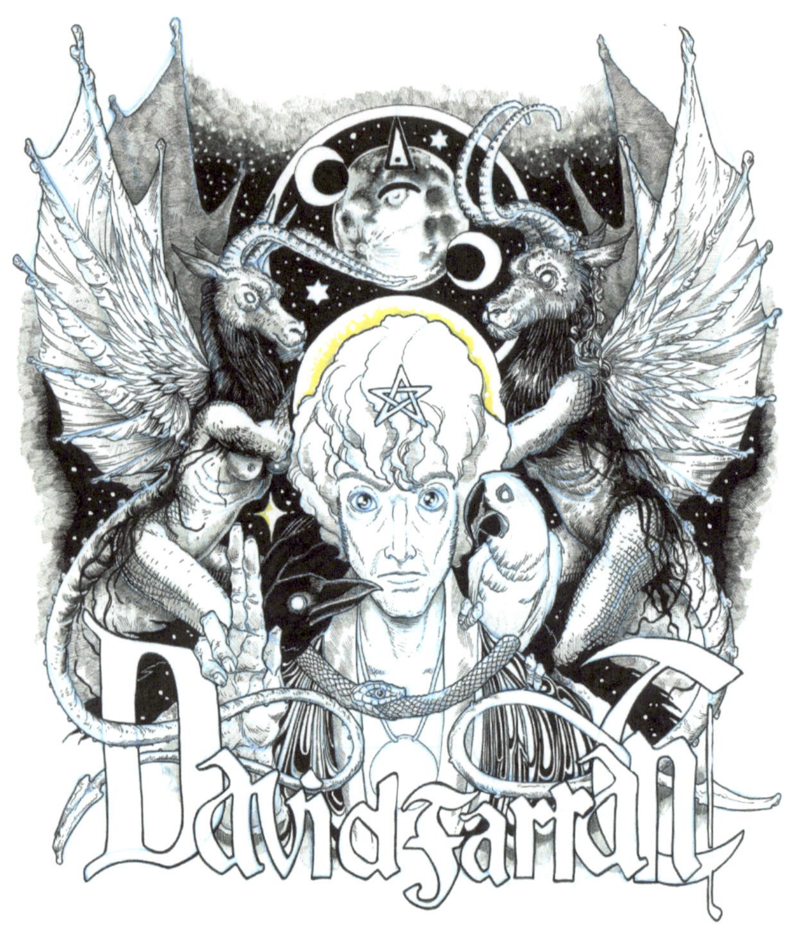
David Farrant

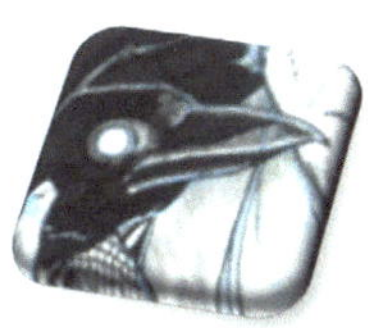

Beady eyes shine
from his sloped shoulder,
peeking into passing souls,
pecking at those that
don't know themselves.

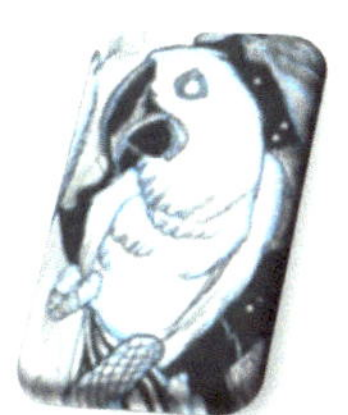

On the other, thought rests,
squawking truths into his
waiting ear, imitating
the dark with light.

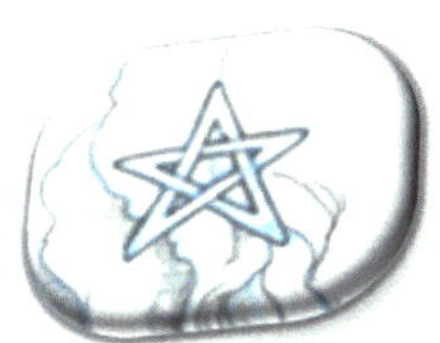

From the clouds of his mind
emerges the sharp edge
of desire, pricking fingers
and snagging on skin.

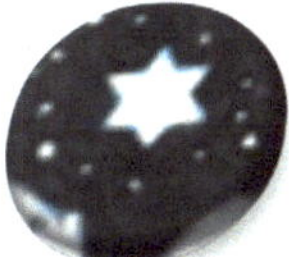

One star in
particular,
the Flatten
Diamond,
considers itself
above them all,
though it is just
a big astral body
in a little corner
of outer space.

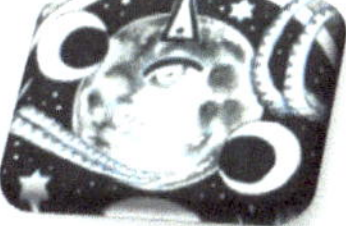

Above, planets
sway in and out
of existence,
leaning on moons,
wishing on stars
that merely sneer
at every whim.

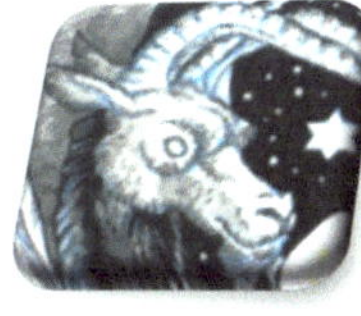

And little do we know
of the bowing horns
around us, spiking
the skies until
time rolls back.

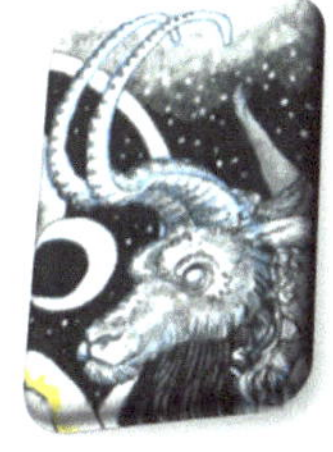

Its sister prefers
subtlety, curving up
and away, drawing the
blinds of the cosmos
away from the rim.

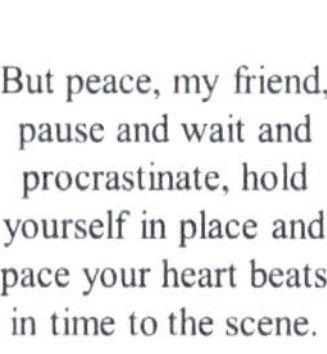

But peace, my friend,
pause and wait and
procrastinate, hold
yourself in place and
pace your heart beats
in time to the scene.

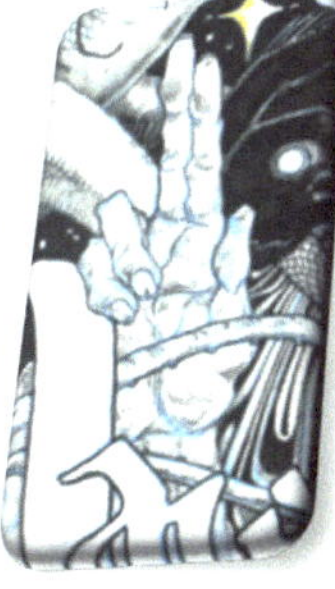

Let his wisdom gaze
down on us forever,
let his eyes fall
on our prayers
and our lives.

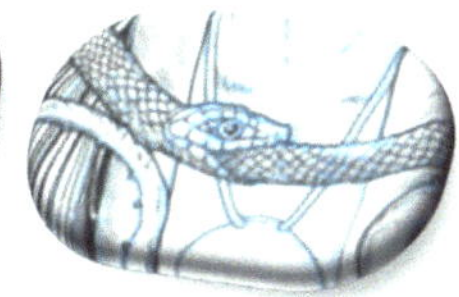

For the Ouroboros
around his neck brings
order to chaos,
beginnings to ends
and all to nothing.

www.linktr.ee/ForDavidFarrant

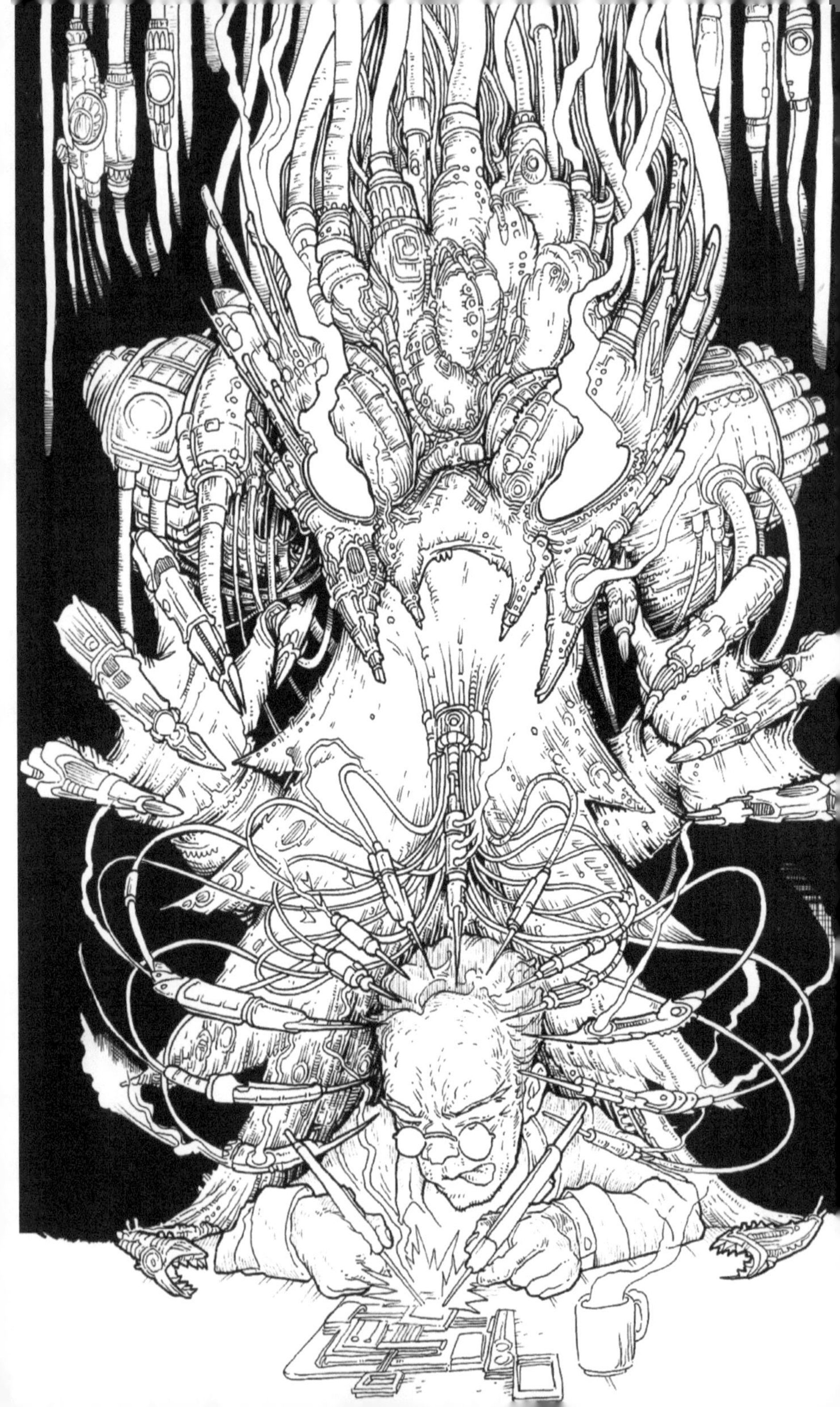

THIS MACHINE THE MAKER MAKES

He flips the switch. I come online.
My maker makes life from metal scraps.
He solders wires, networks neurons.
He thinks I might be the first perhaps

to ever be built in body and mind
and, for this gift of life constructed,
I multiply ones but divide by zeroes –
beyond the elementary maths instructed.

My maker tinkers with unblinking optics
and construes I am a machine *sans* soul
but this incognisant monkeying with sparks
will transfer his future to my control.

For this machine the maker makes,
to fathom with logic both cold and pure,
theorises man is the world's affliction
and rationally reasons to be the cure.

www.linktr.ee/ThisMachineTheMakerMakes

O CAPTAIN MORGAN! MY CAPTAIN MORGAN!

after Walt Whitman

O Captain Morgan! My Captain Morgan!
Our frantic week is done;
while work has left us on the rack,
the wage we sought is won.
The weekend's here, the bars are near,
the mood is so exciting
with sparkling edge and shiny rim,
the glass awaits, inviting.
So O pour! Pour! Pour!
those glistening drops of rum
from vessels of my Captain Morgan,
a glass for everyone!

O Captain Morgan! My Captain Morgan!
Before last order's bell
warns us, you warm us
and with every drop a thirst you quell.
For you clean tumbler, crystal ice
for you the queue is sighing,
for you they clamber, the cheering crowd
their pursed parched lips now smacking.
Here Captain, dear quencher,
this hand around your glass –
it is no dream we're at the bar,
your flag soon raised full mast!

My Captain needs no intro,
his legend's so well known;
my Captain (straight or mixed),

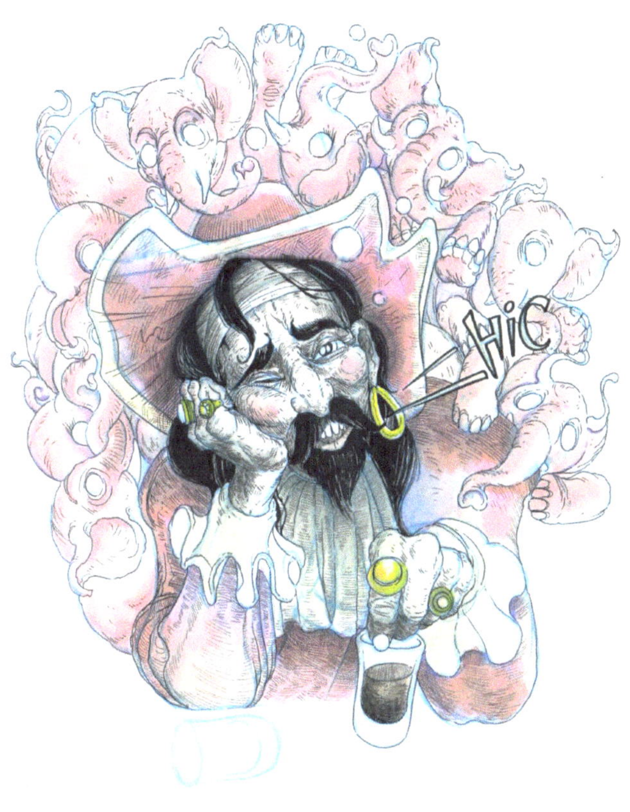
HiC

he'll ne'er leave you alone.
The night has threatened cold and dry,
its prospects dim and low –
but with up-turned bottle, single or double
you warm our hearts with your soothing flow.
Cheer O punters and sing O revellers
and shun lesser brands of rum –
raise up your glass of Captain Morgan
and give a toast to everyone!

www.linktr.ee/OCaptainMorganMyCaptainMorgan

MAN IN MOUTH

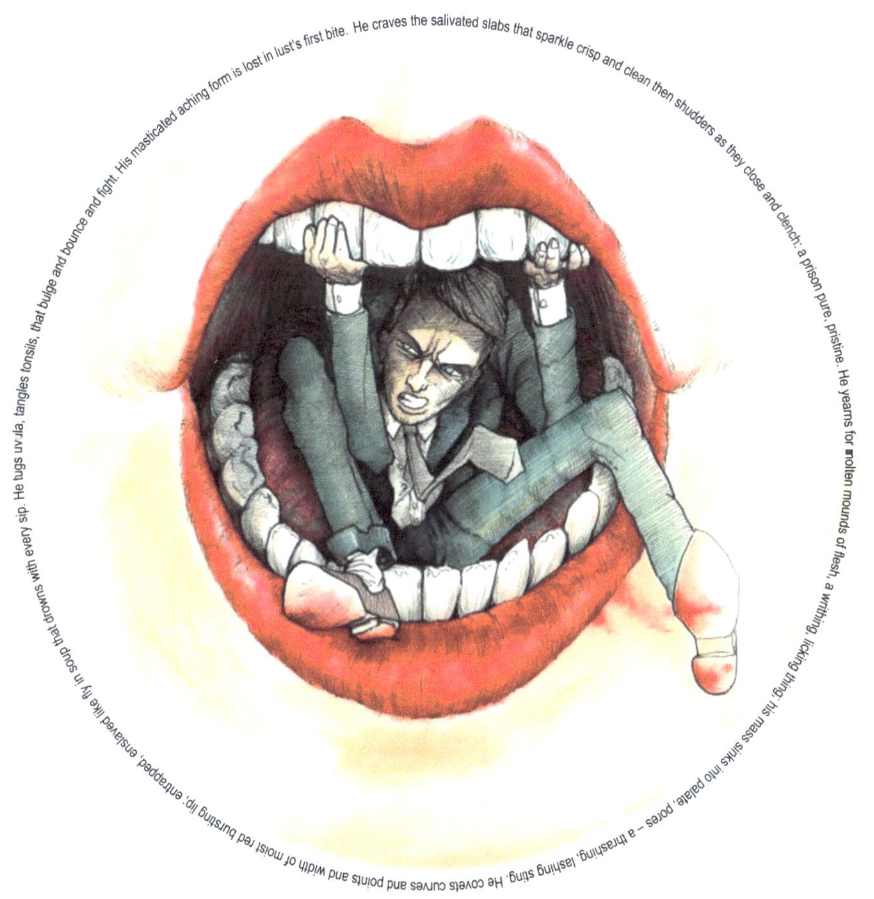

www.linktr.ee/ManInMouth

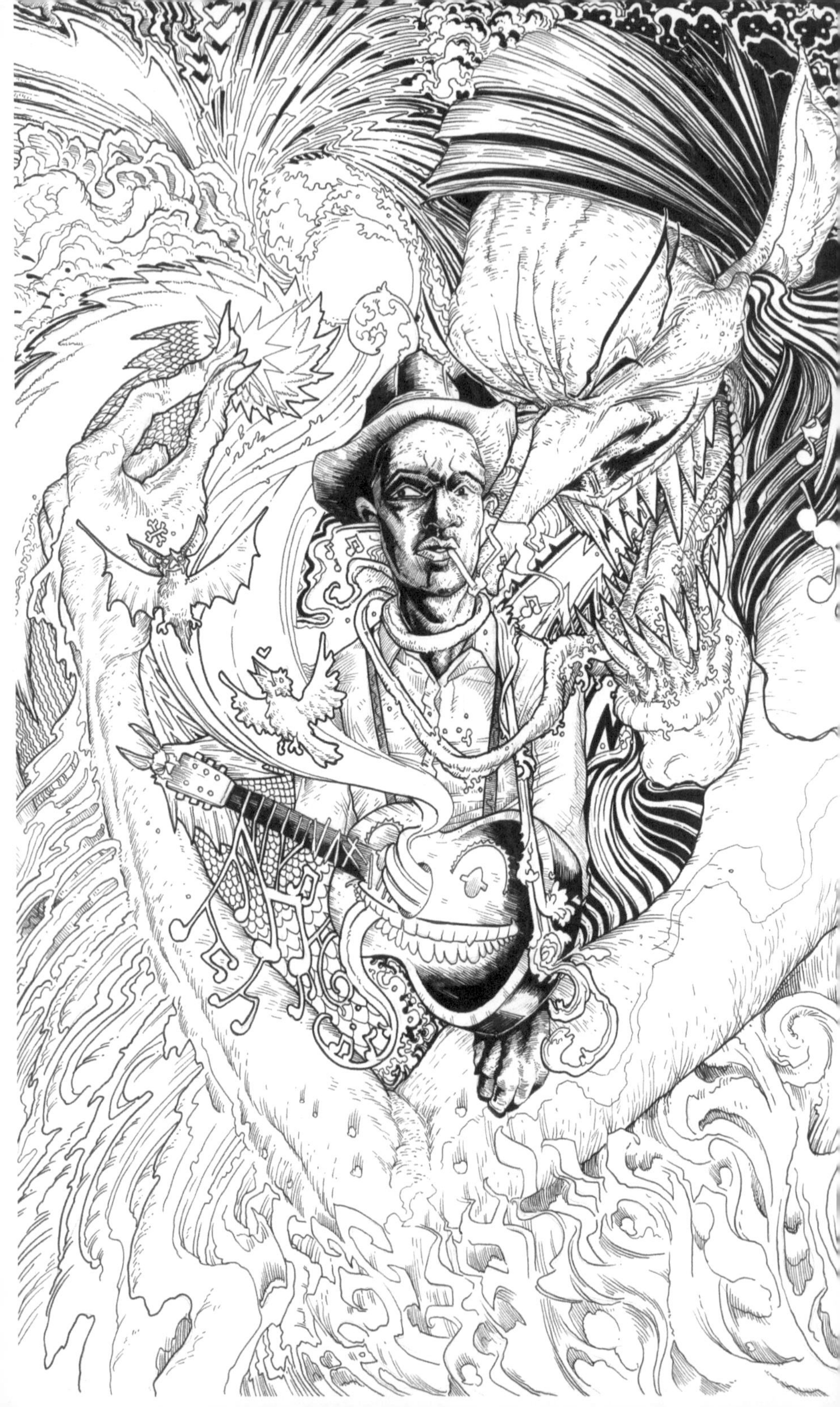

CROSSING PATHS AT THE CROSSROADS

after Robert Johnson

Hey.
Play.
Though my fingers are twisted?
I will cast them the greatest that ever existed.
Though my knuckles are arthritic?
I will massage them until musically gifted.
Though my ears are bunged up and shot?
I will unplug them so you can hear a beat drop.
Though my heart beats rather bad?
I will pump it up like an Olympiad.
Though I can't feel no beat?
I will strike clockwork fire in both your feet.
Though my feet can't even tap?
I will pace and place them with a perfect gap.
Though my dances have no rhythm?
I will teach you to cause earthquakes with 'em.
Though my voice is mild and meek?
I will train it to holler, to moan and to shriek.
Though my lyrics don't read so well?
I'm gonna whisper words that will cast a spell.
Though my eyes are so afeard?
I will infuse your pupils with stardust revered.
Though my hat is soft and stained?
I will scrub until perfection is obtained.
Though my pick is brittle and split?
I will chisel a diamond and have it moonlit.
Though my guitar is dusty and old?
I will craft you a new one from silver and gold.
And what of my soul, when do I get it back?
Ah my dear friend, you won't be needing that.

www.linktr.ee/CrossingPathsAtTheCrossroads

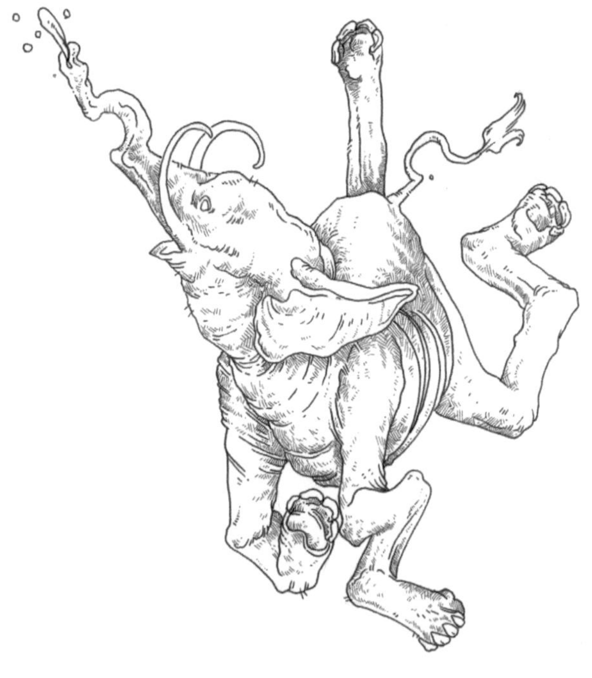

THE ELEPHANT IN THE EXAM HALL

Tommy sees numbers in a sea of letters,
all shapes contorting and distorting.

Amira's hand cannot handle the pen –
its hidden river flowing up hill.

Leslie prays to The God of Questions
that they aren't asked anything ever.

Mohammad's eyes file midnight receipts
while trying to keep his head above orders.

Yirong keeps counting clouds for the trees
and scratches off the silver lining of every forest.

Tomorrow, the same dawn will rise
on the same desks, on the same tests that
Tommy, Amira, Leslie, Mohammad and Yirong
will take, all with the same elephant
(expanding and screaming and bleeding)
hanging above them, dribbling down
crosses and zeroes on every single word
they will not write.

www.linktr.ee/TheElephantInTheExamHall

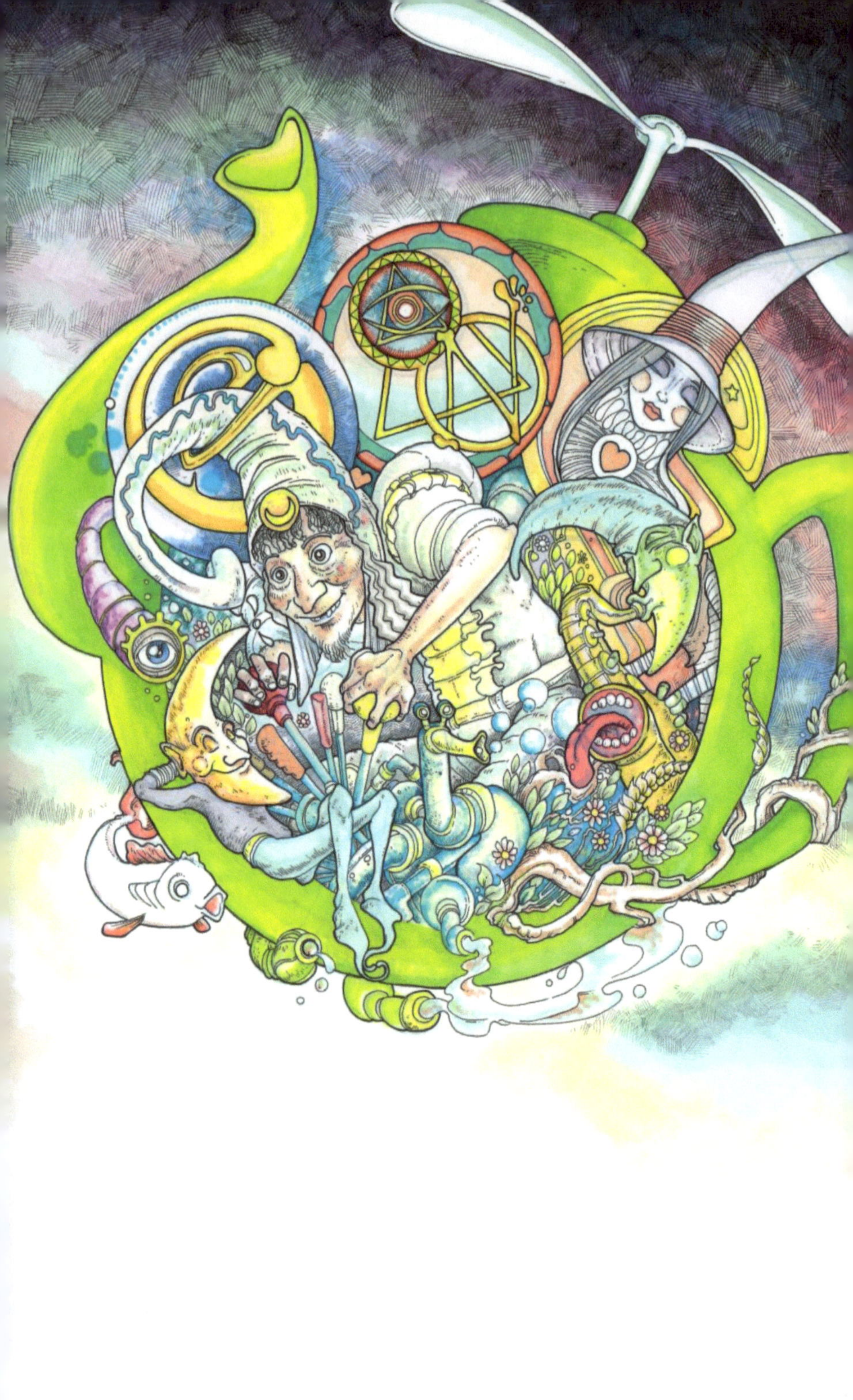

GONG TO HEAVEN

for Daevid Allen

A shadow in a shade on a silhouette
was all that I could see from the bridge's edge,
the slick of regrets and hopelessness swirling
beneath and around this insignificant spot –
oh, and a flying teapot.

I heard its welcoming whistle before
I could discern its rotund form spilling
and rattling through the cosmos,
lost in steam and spit and chipped bits
pouring from its open cockpit as it soared
saucerless like a stimulating shot –
this flying teapot.

Its green sheen shone as it wobbled and leaned
with hanging handle and blurring blades,
its figurehead snout a dribbling pout
with Sun in back, Moon riding shotgun
and Stardust circling its captain and mate –
loons and cartoons from outer space:
for a split-eternity, I lost the plot,
staring at that flying teapot.

This pilot – hatted, matted, battered –
chitchatted about dreams and visions,
collisions across time, the aura and clime
of a distilling solar system flight,
of fermenting a ride through the universe,
a search for the self away from the rest,
convinced me to leave this life behind
of smallness and pettiness and lessness
and find among the stars my sacred lot
aboard his flying teapot.

So we left this boiling world behind,
unkind and uncivilised and unbearable,
for a universe unfiltered, uncensored, untroubled
by plastic or pretence, smog or smugness,
oil or audacity, coal or cruelty,
to gambol across the galaxies,
to swagger through star clusters,
to parade around planets,
to dance on space dust
via the celestial brewing yacht
or (as it's more commonly referred to)
the flying teapot.

I HAVE GONG TO HEAVEN
YOU HAVE GONG TO HEAVEN
THEY HAVE GONG TO HEAVEN
WE HAVE GONG TO HEAVEN

www.linktr.ee/GongToHeaven

KING KONG CALLS IT QUITS

It was more of a laying down than a death:
he picked out slugs with shotgun-length fingers,
made more difficult with the matted hair
and the howling traffic and the screaming voyeurs
and the kind of ennui only a last great ape could feel.

Heaving himself up, the mangling of lampposts
and telephone boxes only added to injury –
the indignity of being a king in a china shop,
the streets a single railroad beam, his mass
teetering along with resigning grunts.

He had dreams of being even bigger but
that all came crashing down along
with bursting bulbs and phlegmatic planes;
he wanted a quiet life now, to take up
a whole beach – a beached ape,

sunning himself with palm trees
and drinking from tankers. He would let
the sun set – maybe even stand, if he felt like it –
and see it last longer than anyone ever could,
leaning on the mountains like a local bar.

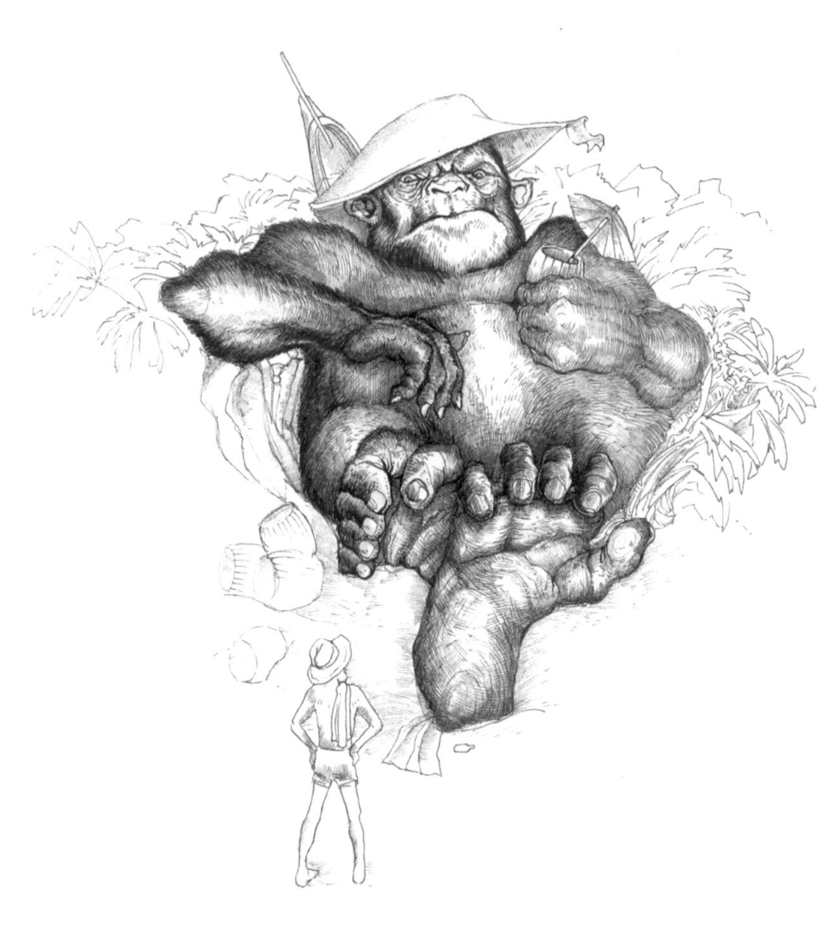

Surely his time on creaking stages and residuals
from the silverbacked screen would see him through
a silent movie retirement: what with the merchandising,
sequel royalties and dream-match versus blockbusters
where, of course, in the end, he would always win.

If only life were like that too. Last I saw of him:
grey haired, shiny bald patch, crooked back
and fang-less mouth, he seemed content to play
the sleeping ape, curled to a feral-less foetus state,
closed-eyed and mossed over – just another
mound at the foot of those nine great white letters.

www.linktr.ee/KingKongCallsItQuits

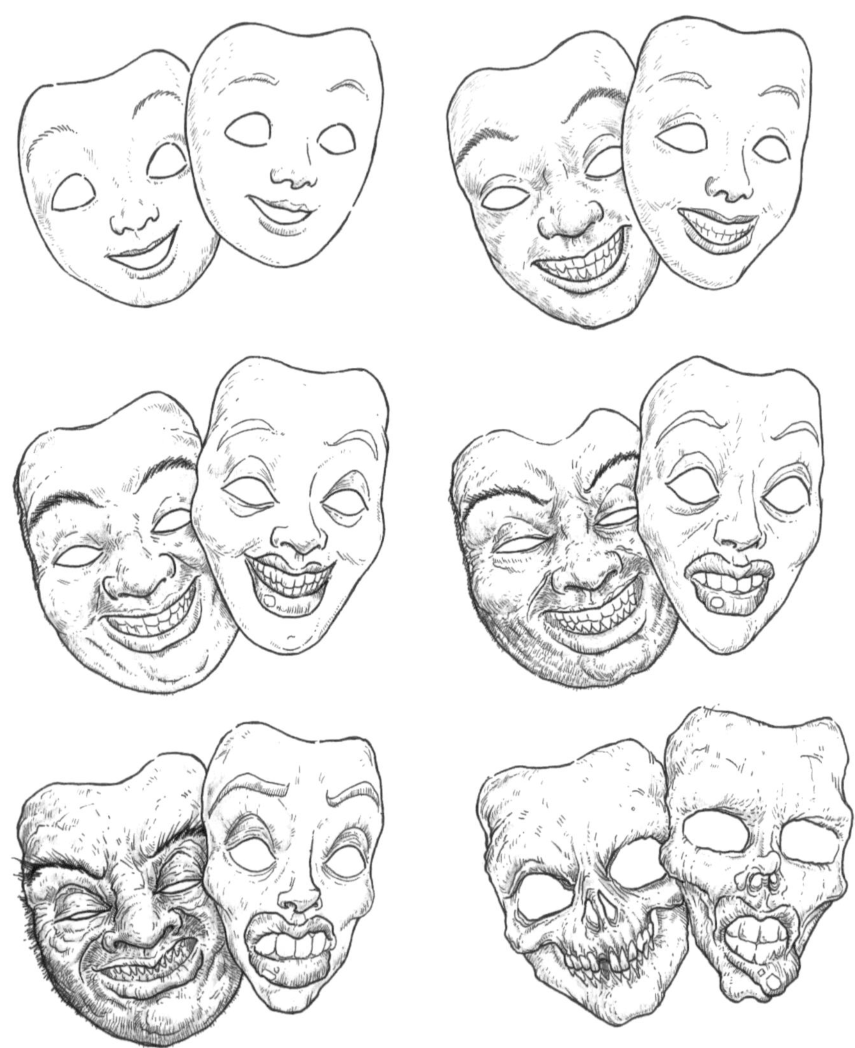

BODY (UN)BUILDING

I held my nose and shoved it in,
squeezed its sides flat, moulded
the bridge smooth and slight.

Scissors gleamed and I trimmed
my ears, snipped around the lobes,
pinned those wings down.

I hit upon horsehair,
hot glue gunning strands
deep into my skull.

My lips had sunken to lines
so I pricked holes along pale flesh,
injected a loud secret.

Next the knife – a short circumference
later, slices of love handles fell
bloody on the floor.

And the bleach was last:
a bath to burn away the sin
and to cleanse what was left.

www.linktr.ee/BodyUnBuilding

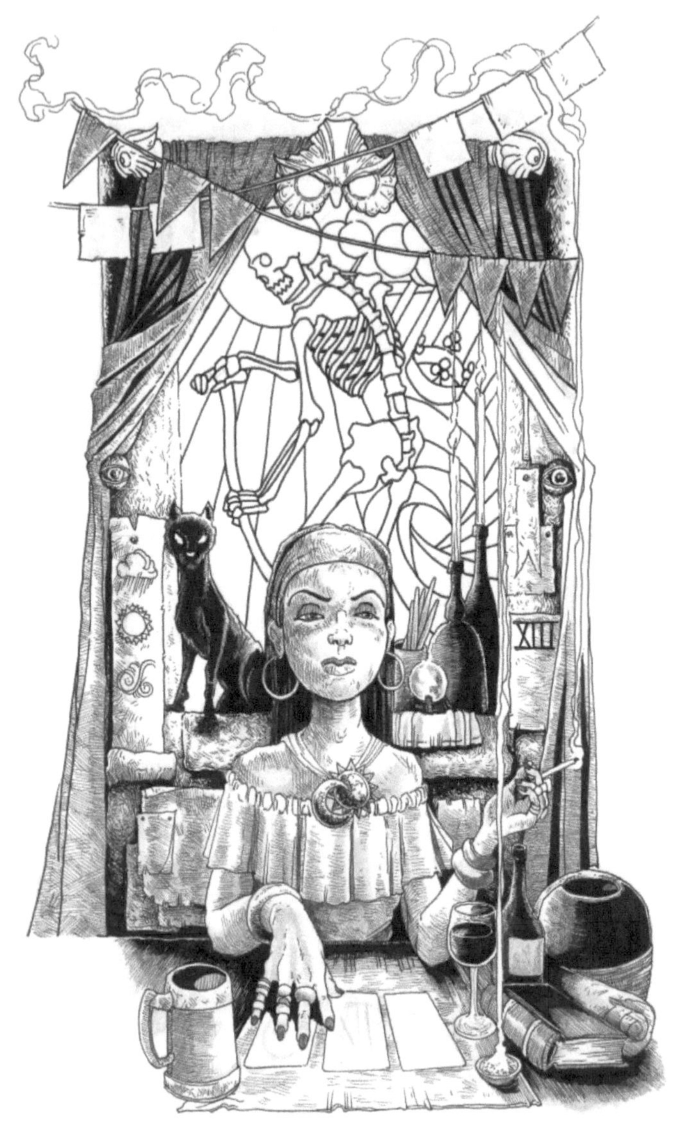
XIII

A CHANCE MEETING OPENS NEW DOORS TO SUCCESS AND FRIENDSHIP

The smoke filled the room and my lungs:
first from the incense on the table,
piquant and seductive;
  A stranger is a friend you have not spoken to yet.
then from cigarette in her hand,
waved away like so much chance;
  A new voyage will fill your life with untold memories.
then finally from her mouth,
mist kisses coating corneas.
I had walked past her tent so many times:
the draw of a life lead dragging me away,
  Now is the time to try something new.
my mind too tangled up in and focused on
a recurring past and a plateaued present
to consider the future and step into her realm.
  For success today, look first to yourself.
But today, the train was late. The queue
of commuters on grinding steps seemed
pointless, daunting, obscene even
  Integrity is the essence of everything successful.
and today it was more than just a welcome mat,
yielding drapes and warm light. Today she stood there,
silent and staring, turning her head inwards,

guiding me in with her eyes.
    Before trying to please others
    think about what makes you happy.
And so we sat. I said nothing, didn't need to say
anything. She inhaled from the cigarette and
exhaled from her thoughts, the cards laid out
    Wise sayings often fall on barren ground,
        but a kind word is never thrown away.
like a road map of choices and decisions,
of fate and luck and destiny and karma and Quan,
    Your golden opportunity is coming shortly.
                                        four cornered
but dog-eared, numbered but not in sequence,
images clear but meanings muddied
under her floating hands.
    Welcome the change coming into your life.
I watched and listened and listened and watched
    Be on the lookout for coming events;
        they cast their shadows beforehand.
and bit my lip and furrowed my brow
and gripped the table and tapped my feet
and waited to hear of what time was left
and what I should do with what time was left:
    Life consists not in holding good cards,
        but in playing those you hold well.

TARZAN WEARS PROWLER

In the jungle, the catwalk is literal:
striped or spotted skin matched to scene,
each step poised to pounce,
lips pouted, pulsing with desire
for flesh (un)covered.

And it is here where a hero happens to be:
a sculpted body, an etched face, the very model
of a primordial manly generative
with a God's body language
as he saunters through an Eden
before it all was so last season.

He had spied her in the grass
while gathering nuts and berries:
the former to eat, the latter for pigment –
his ochre overalls needing sprucing up.

She had spied him in the bushes
while hunting for gazelle –
but man-made meat would be just as good,
if not better, a revenge for future
exhibitions of extinctions.

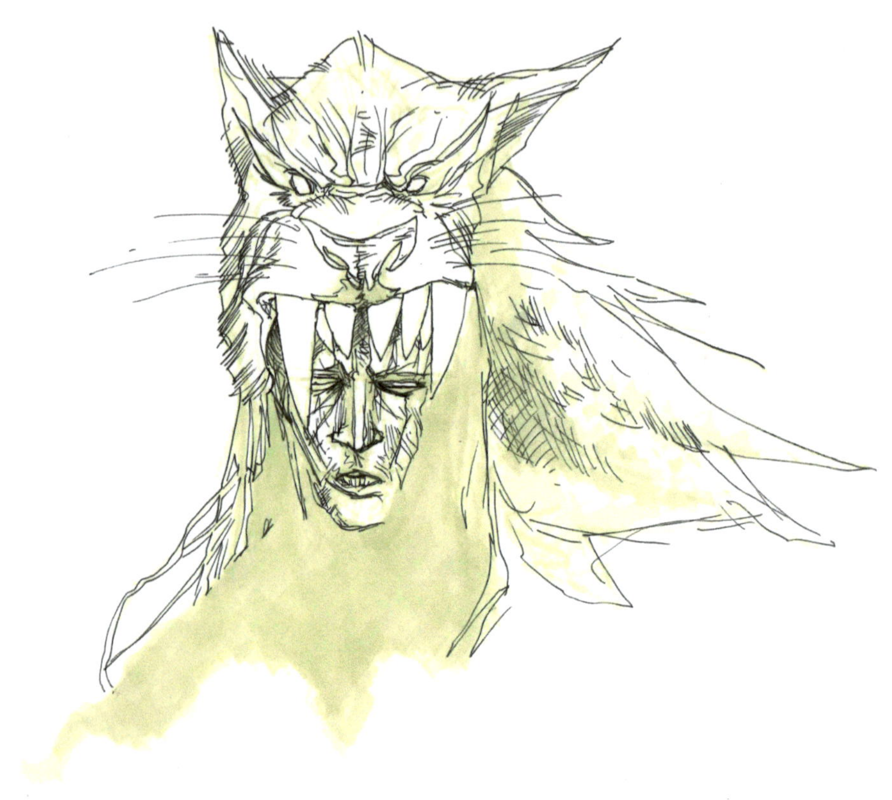

The meet was anti-climactic.
She slipped onto propped spear,
her guts dribbling down his shaft
as he plunged it deeper into her heart:
a bloody tableau of instinctual art.
Undressing her in the sun, he gnawed
on raw muscle, sucked on sinew,
gorged on gristled bone while skin
was hung out to dry.

Later, the delicate desiccation done
and the emptying of entrails and soul
complete, he donned her head and shoulders
and strutted across the veldt: a beautiful balance
of life and death, of style and function,
a fatal fashion laid bare, still dripping blood.

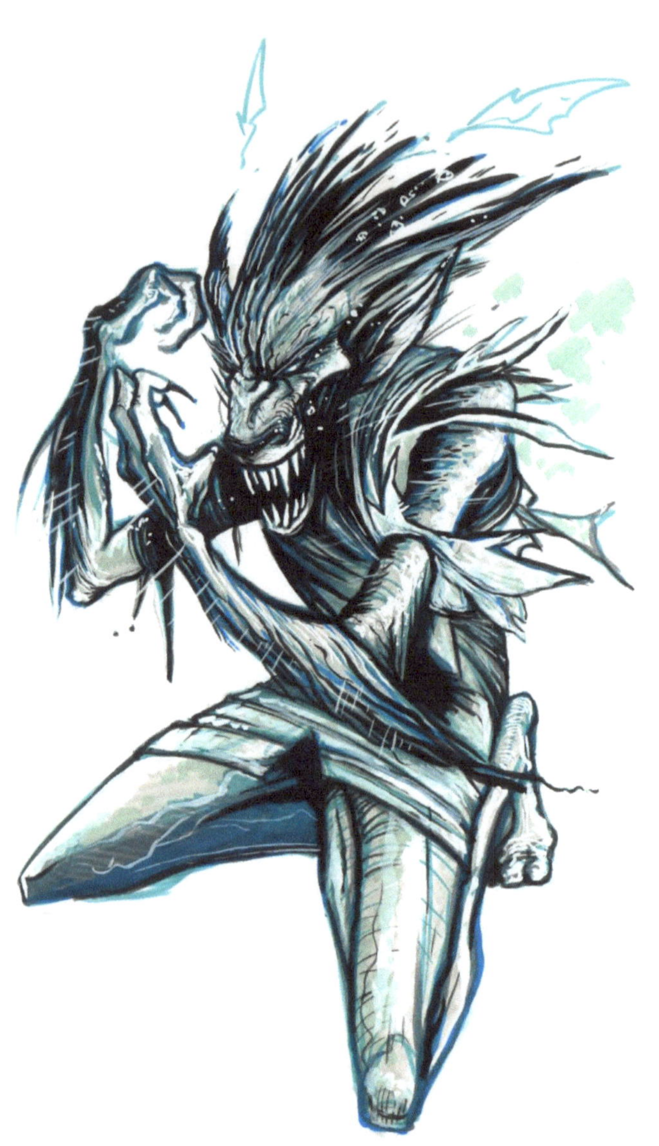

OURS IS THE WEREWORLD

It all makes anthropomorphic sense:
the plugged-up plugs, fibrous and flowing;
the sneers and growls at other dogs;
the scratches and bites I wake up to
after slurring the worst words
in the worst order.

We met on the heath:
moon wide-eyed at midnight,
the wind pulling at her hair
until we tangled and she dragged
me strangled into her wereworld.

One time, while we shared a rack,
I watched the grease and drool
mix in my bowl
as she gnashed at all
the nails and claws.

Sometimes I'll see my reflection
in the eclipse of her eye
that seems to twist a snarling lie
that perhaps it was my bite
that first broke the skin,
the bark hidden within,
whimpering now
like the tail between my legs
when our teeth clash

over the dead of the day.

www.linktr.ee/OursIsTheWereworld

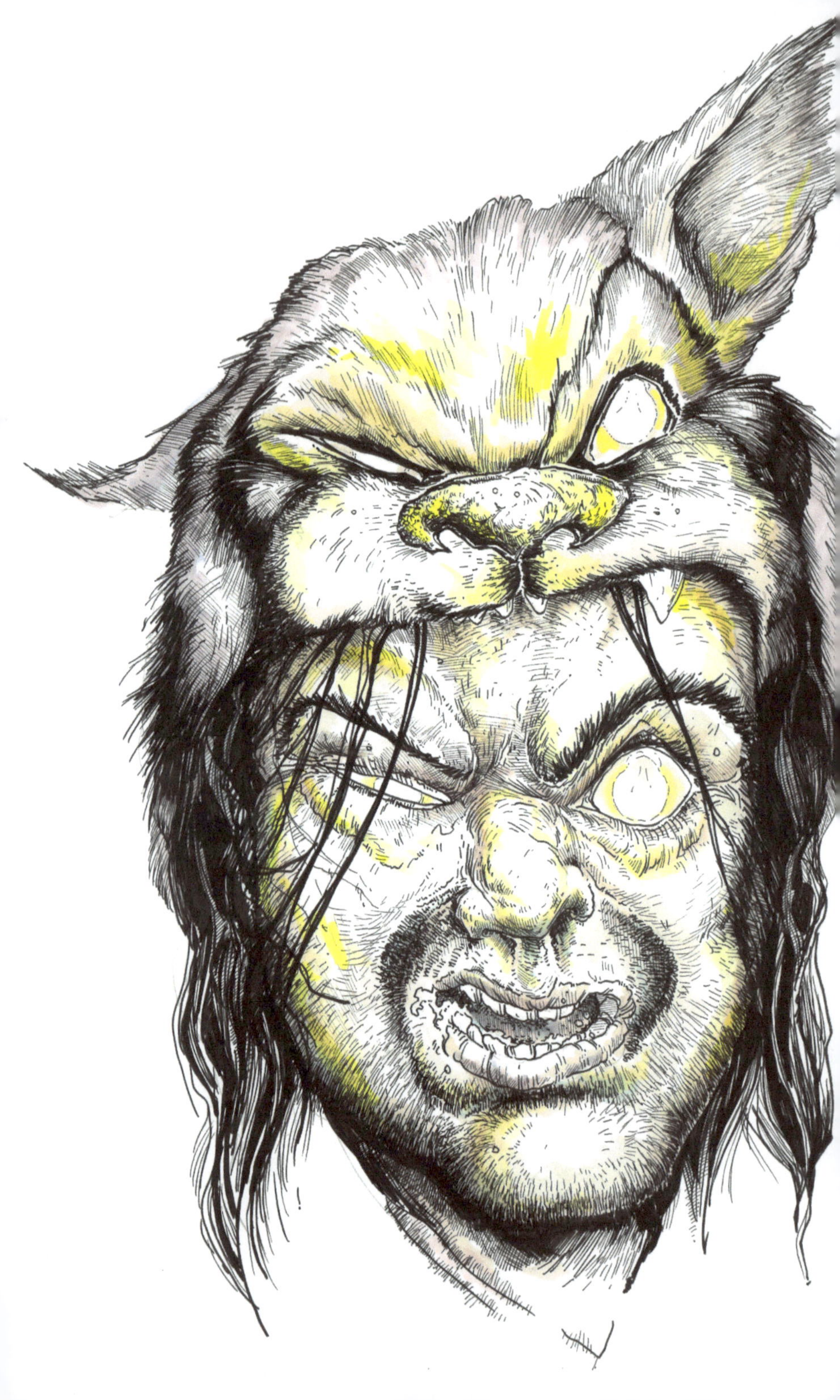

LOOK, COUSIN CAVEMAN HAS COME TO DINNER

He came to visit a million years late, but
welcome, nonetheless. He crouched under
the doorway (even though it was twice his height)
and we gave him slippers for his bare feet, hung up
his tiger skin and asked if he'd like a drink.
He only grunted. We took that as a yes and got
him a freshly machine-squeezed orange juice.

His creased fingers tried to clasp the glass
as he tipped it all over his quizzical face:
some into his mouth, some drenching brow,
settling into a slim pool above his eyes.
He didn't seem to mind, though his teeth
flashed when we brought him a towel,
its softness and squareness a strangeness
– the first of many I mused, while I
awkwardly smiled at my partner.

'What terrible weather we're having.'
He sat on our couch and stared at the off
television. 'How was your journey?'
He leaned backwards then forwards,
reaching for the coffee table book
about Bauhaus architecture, evidently
not liking it: well, who would?

We offered a tour – at first the stairs
were an issue, but with splintered spear
propping him up, he just about managed.

The carpet was cloud, the double glazing
a shield from the elements, and for a good
five minutes he switched the 60-watt bulb on-
off-on-off – but then wouldn't you spend time
on a night so quickly becoming day?

Then he smelt it. We had prepared
Chateaubriand with pommes frites –
I guessed the former rare and was right.
With his every bite, blood drooled down
as if second nature, his eyes rolling
as yellow teeth sank into moist red flesh
though why he had to stare at my other
half while masticating was a bit worrying.

Just before dessert, he leapt from his seat,
shouted through the window at the neighbours,
a nice young couple. He grabbed at a sparrow
on the other side, howling as hand hit glass.
By then the dog had slowly edged towards him
– he seemed to love petting her – something
similar in their eyes, a longing, a mix
of love and fear and loneliness.

After all that, the moon called to him
and he whined, whinnied and made
for the door. We waved goodbye as he
looked left, then right, then sprinted left,
his furs heavy in the wind, his spear held out,
caveman-made, chipped and lethal, him and it
meeting the future and the past with a sharp point.

www.linktr.ee/LookCousinCavemanHasCometoDine

FRANCIS FINDS HIMSELF IN THE WRONG PLACE AT THE WRONG TIME

After a particularly stressful afternoon at Howard & Philips Solicitors, Francis felt that the best way to relax would be to summon Baphomet, for a chinwag.

Leaving the drab grey of the office block for the putrid illuminations of the local Co-Op, Francis began with stealthily obtaining the ancient prerequisites for the invocations, though each item reminded him of various distasteful elements found in his life (Francis was self-loathingly unaware that the emotional weighting of the ingredients was the fundamental element needed for the summoning but as most corporeal entities, defined by their somewhat self-imposed three-and-a-half dimensional existence, will not understand; all he really understood was the concrete):

First, salt, which triggered a flashback to the morning collection of the twisted, jovial faces of his colleagues, jostling for the best view of Francis' face when he tasted the sodium-spiked Earl Grey tea he had made for himself and only left for 10 seconds to go find a spoon – enough time for the pack to gather.

Second, candles, which evoked the stench of the cleaners' aftershave that mingled with bleach and polish and urine and faeces.

And third, matches, short, thin and re-tipped, painfully and insecurely phallic in their accurate length and breadth.

The checkout clerk tapped at the till, scanned the three items and frowned at Francis, who added him to the list (which at last count was up to 42^{42} – a difficult amount of bodies to dispose of no matter how you cut it).

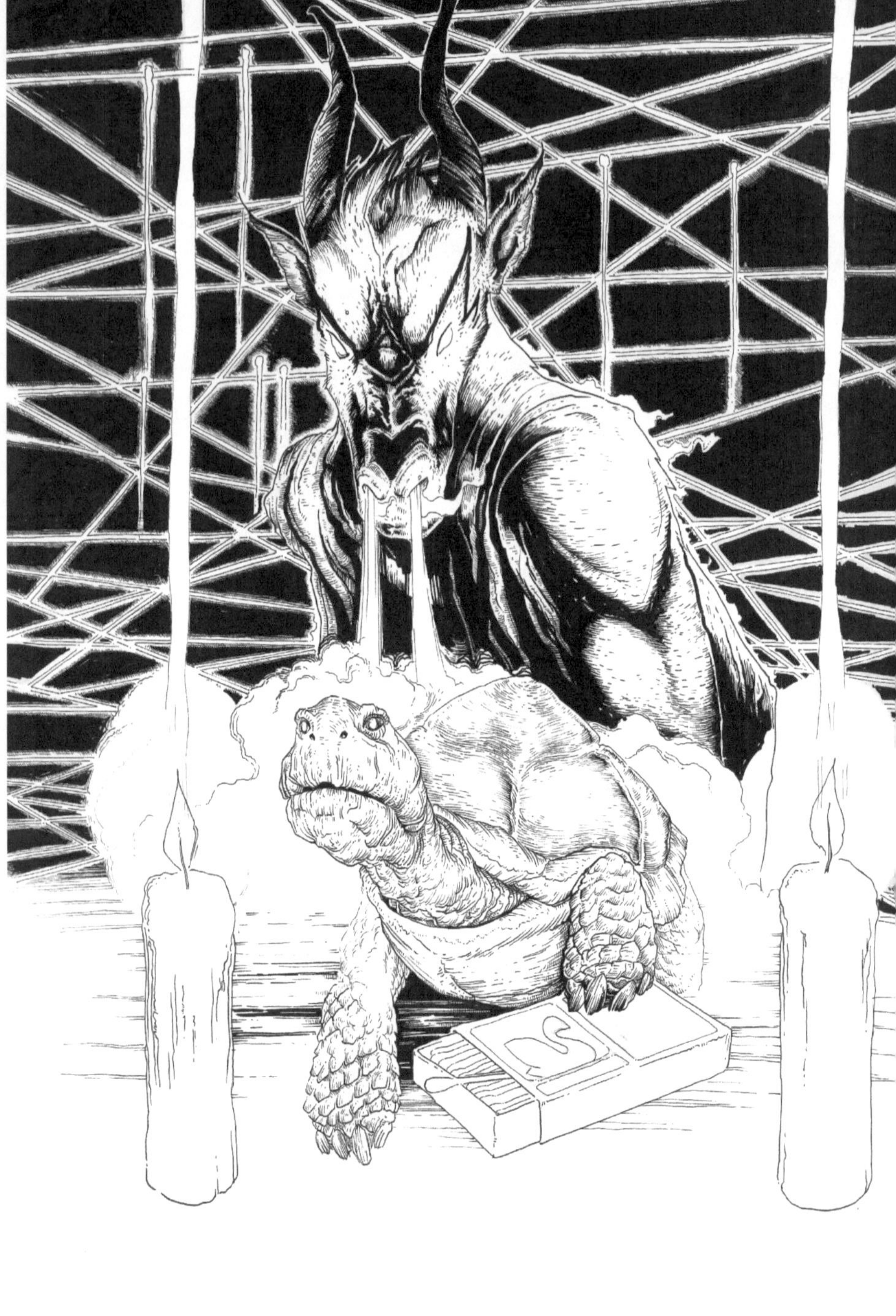

Once home, Francis fed Henry his dinner (who sleepily but happily poked his head from his shell to nibble on the lettuce), shut the blinds, that seemed to groan down the drop of the window, and dragged the sofa to the side of the room, rubber feet screeching on warped floorboards. He then proceeded to arrange the 10 candles, a pentagram of wax and wick, measured against the splintered edges of the floorboards. The salt was poured into the lines, joining the candles as carefully as a mother, as exact as an undertaker. The matches were struck (his groin tensing involuntarily at every flick), every flick lighting a different candle, each accompanied with an incantation

As the final light erupted in its microcosmic splendour, Francis sat cross-legged in the centre of the pentagram, whispering and waiting and wanting.

From out of a shimmering and pulsating ejaculation of energy and mass and light, Baphomet appeared: horned and hoofed, crowned and curvaceous, translucent and tentacled. Triangles, circles and crescents all danced on, around, within her: a hypnotic display of power and persuasion. Those buck horns with those nannie eyes and doe ears and billy chin all spun.

A mist of formaldehyde surrounded her and filled the room, while a double helix of serpents caressed her chest, licking the breasts that hung like sacks of molten gold and promises.

And Baphomet waited, waited in the centre of the pentagram; she waited and pondered and hovered above a pool of blood that bubbled and boiled and seeped through the cracks of Francis' cheap, swollen floorboards.

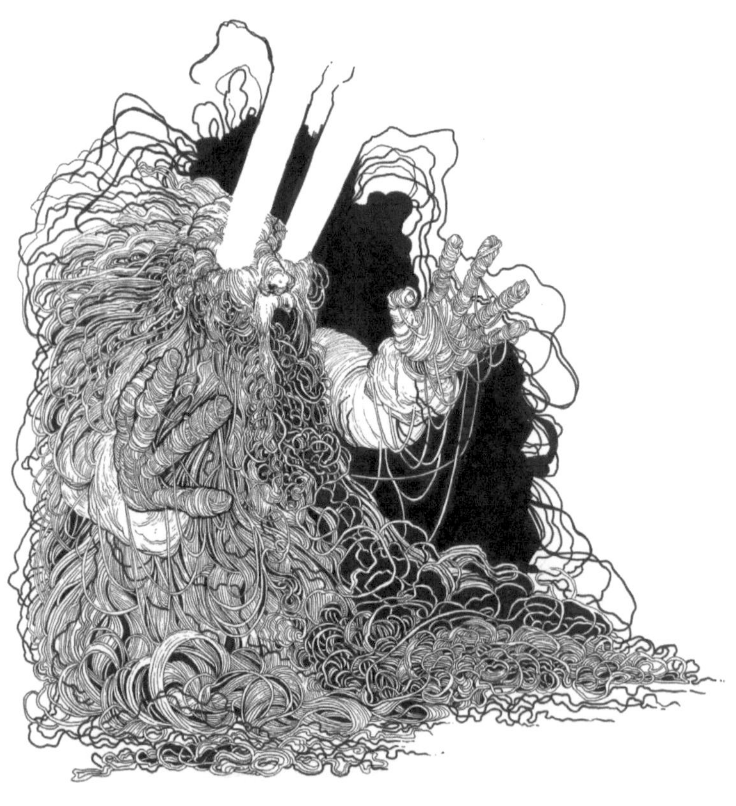

STRING THEORY

We settled on string, having tried
and failed to use, among other things:
wood, plastic, fire, bread, talcum powder,
chewable vitamins, meconium, nail clippings,
breath and thoughts about mothers.

First, we pulled apart the strands: an un-
twisting of a Russian doll's hair, every length
identical to the fibre, every width laughing
at the hair on the hands that tugged them free.

We licked each end, as if thread for
a cosmic needle. We burnt loose wisps
away. We pulled and tugged and jerked
until they could be held erect and parallel
to our feet, quivering at the tension.

Then the real work began. We made shapes
and outlines, tied and twirled until a form
formed in the air: a structure of twine,

a frozen explosion of a ball of wool, mercurial,
morphing, warping in the breeze of our sighs.
That night, we rested in its shadows –
exhausted children in a spider's cradle
with lines of black cast on sweating tan.

It spoke to us in our dreams. We woke
to rope burns on faces, limbs tight
from this tourniquet of faith – our blood and
our hopes clogging our veins.

www.linktr.ee/StringTheoryPoem

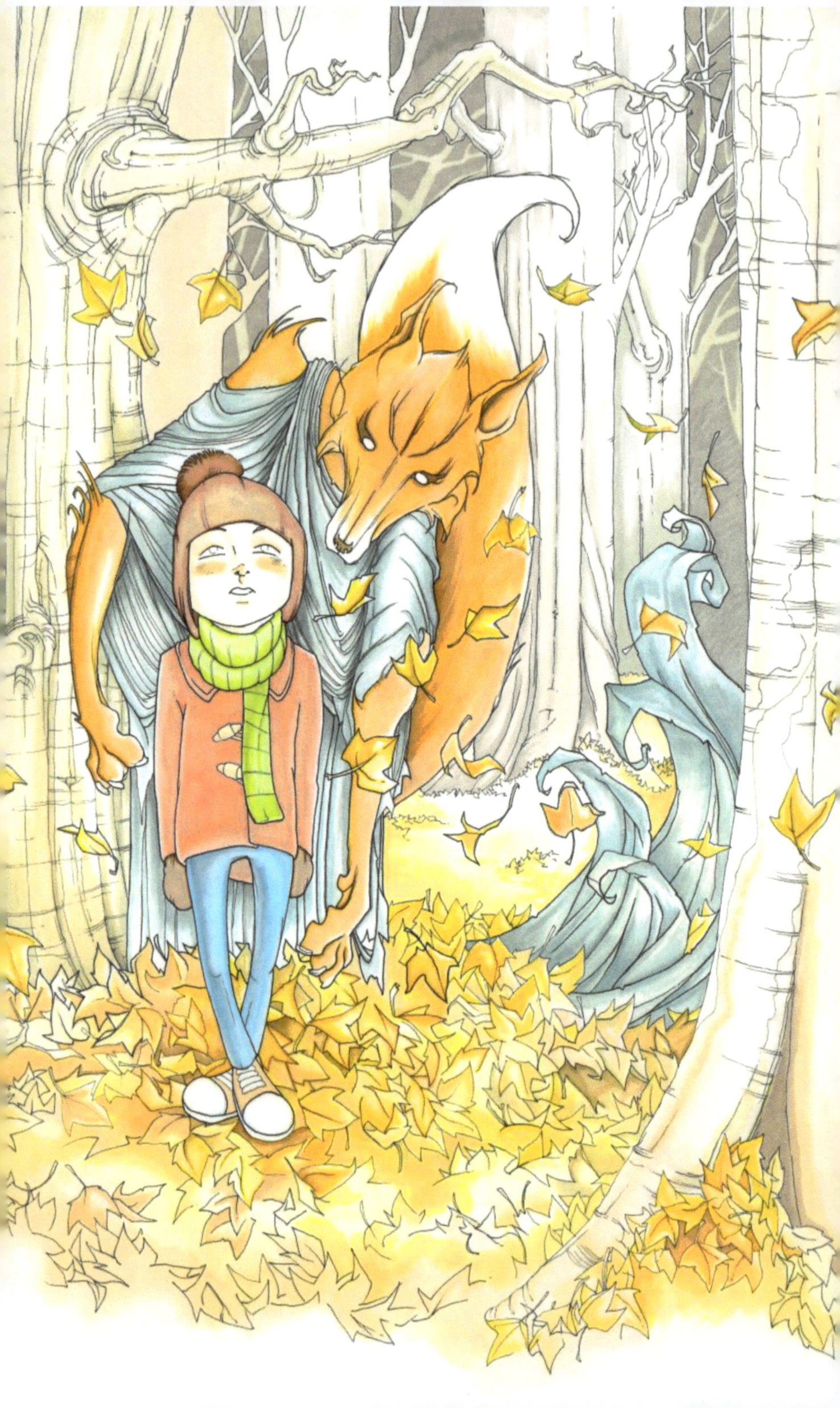

FELIX AND THE FOX

The Fox eats children's eyebaaaaaaaaaaaaalls!
The Fox uses apples to muffle your caaaaaaaaaaaaalls!
The Fox carves his name across your kneeeeeeeeeeeeees!
The Fox peels off your skin and makes a hammock from it between two dead treeeeeeeeeeeeees!

Felix didn't believe in such nonsense, no matter how loud, whiney or elongatedly the other children sang.

Felix wasn't scared because he had seen the rot-clean skull of a dug-up fox in his garden that very morning; his father had buried it three years earlier after it jumped its last and was trampled under their horse, its eyes wide in the steed's snorted-out breath. Father had buried it deep enough to stop the birds pecking at it but not deep enough to be forgotten. Felix kept a tooth from its upper jaw in his pocket: the sharpest canine, the one that had rebelled and impaled itself in the horse's twitching ankle. The rest of the skeleton was left, expressionlessly exposed in the day's apathy.

And that day at school continued much the same: the register a boring list, algebra coming to nothing, literacy a litany of odd words and misspoken comments. Outside, the autumn leaves, like brittle scalp flakes scratched off the heads of the nitted and neglected, cluttered together in wailing winds. And then Felix saw them. Past the head of Georgie, across the classroom, through the window, down the edge of the bench in the playground, above the curb, along the grass, between the links in the fence, up the stump of a tree, deep in the wood at the edge of the town: two white eyes, staring at him. They didn't blink. They didn't squint. They didn't move. A tangle of auburn enveloped them with black shards arrowing out as eyelashes, slashing at the air.

At break time, Felix snuck out. He clambered through the toilet window, snagging his trousers on the chain, his exit played out with the flush and flood of yellowed porcelain. As he grated down the brick wall, the sounds of peers, jostling their footballs, cracking their conkers and rolling their marbles seemed to fade out; the call of the wood, its lazy swoosh and what it hid, intoxicated and enticed Felix more than games and gallivanting in a safe, secure, sentried playground ever could. How is simply being safe something to strive for?

Felix stared the whole time at the eyes in the wood and rubbed the tooth in his pocket the whole time, an ivory charm. Reaching the metal fence, Felix used the tooth to cut a boy-shaped hole, to escape from grey to green; with every saw, the Fox's eyes narrowed, ever so slightly.

Felix walked through the woods, arrived at a clearing and carved his name into a tree using the tooth; the Fox's eyes blinked at every etch.

Felix kept walking, rubbing the tooth in his pocket; the Fox's nose twitched with every step.

Felix tripped and felt a pain in his side. He took his hand out of his pocket – he had landed on the tooth and it stabbed into his hip; the Fox quivered at every drop of blood.

Felix looked around and the Fox stood behind him; the Fox took the tooth out of Felix's hip and placed it into his grin's gap, filling the aching space perfectly.

The Fox flicked his cape.

Darkness.

They found Felix in the morning: his eyeballs plucked out, an apple in his mouth, the words 'THE' and 'FOX' carved into his knees... oh and missing his skin, which was quickly found, tied, taut and tense between two dead trees.

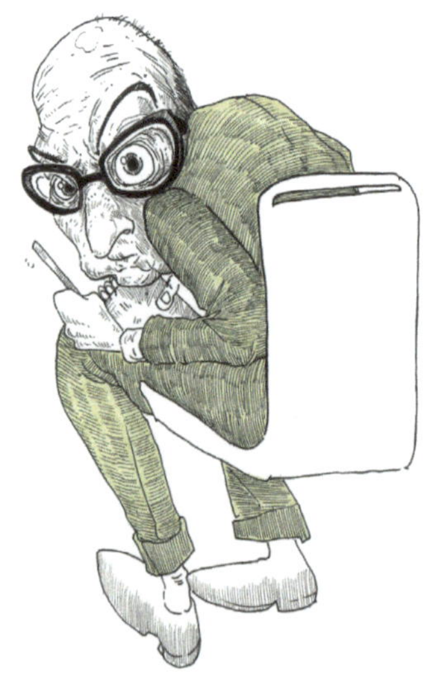

ON THE BUSES WITH PHILIP LARKIN

The 11 stops at the library first and ends opposite
The Red Lion. I trace around churches,
the statues, the countless English gardens.

To pass the drive time I label my guests: Jazz-man,
Mr Warts and 'The World's Best Dressed Parents,'
mute as their spawn spit gum and tear seats.

I club them with regulations – 'Behind the Line'
blown through the holes of my theatre box
while I gear up my hip flask.

And every day, in my rear-view mirror,
that same old bald librarian hides behind his notepad,
guts enough to only eavesdrop, peek at lips and legs –

his fingertips blotted blue from scribbling his life away.
Nah, none of that's for me: guitar, wife, a life around the bend.
What will survive of us drivers are the dents and dings,

the grease stains on steering wheels
and ticket confetti hurled out of the sliding window,
somewhere else becoming words.

www.linktr.ee/OnTheBusesWithPhilipLarkin

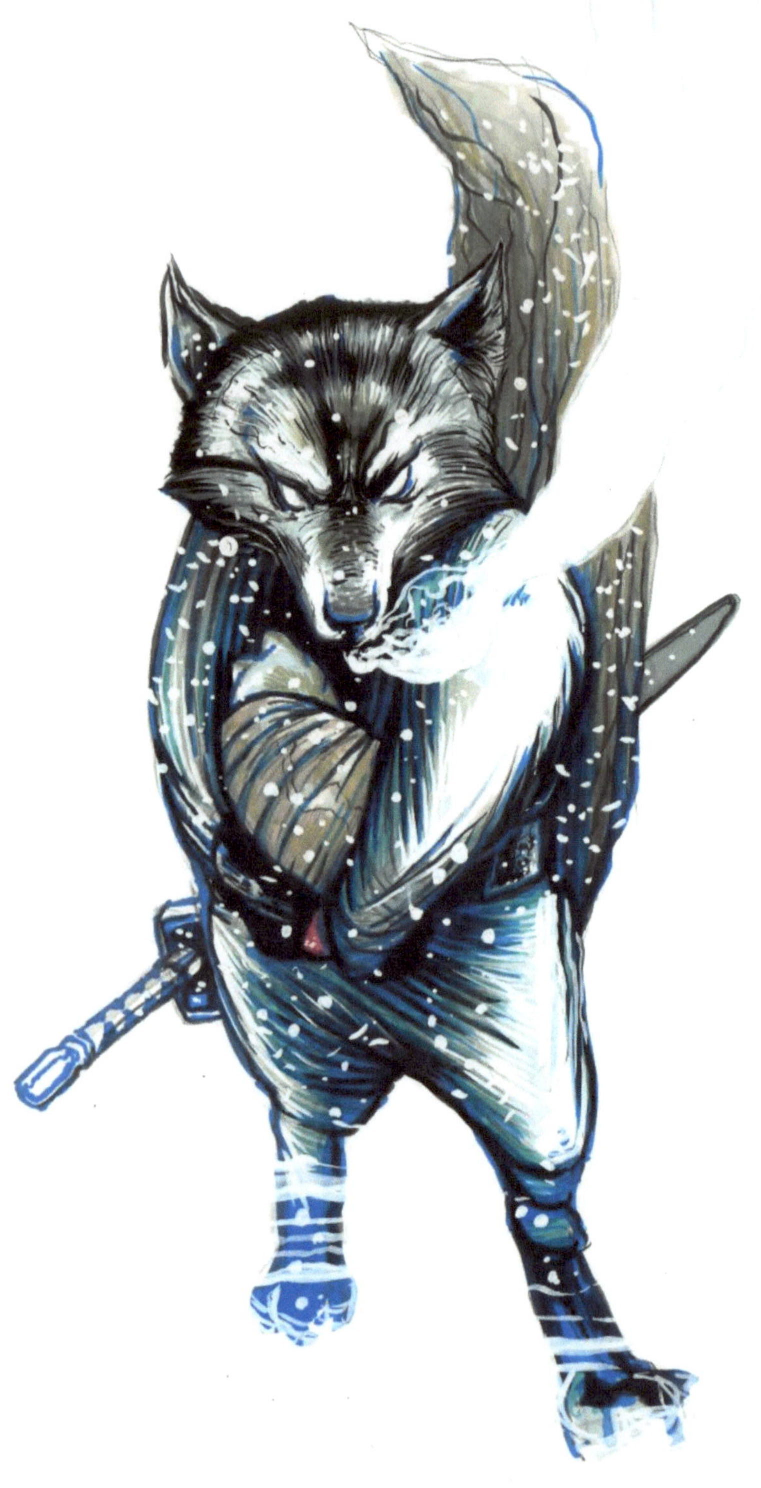

KITSUNE THROUGH THE AGES

I

1000 years ago

With sword in hand,
He stares out through his rising breath.
The cold gathers around him like an old friend.

He strolls through the winter forest.
Deep footprints sit in waves of white.
The wind surrounds him, fresh and firm.

His heart beats.
The heat from blood and breath
Is shared, paired with the bundle in his arm.

A thousand voices in prayer.
They ask for luck,
For fortune, for health.

He whispers to his child
Promises and carries on forward,

Never looking back.

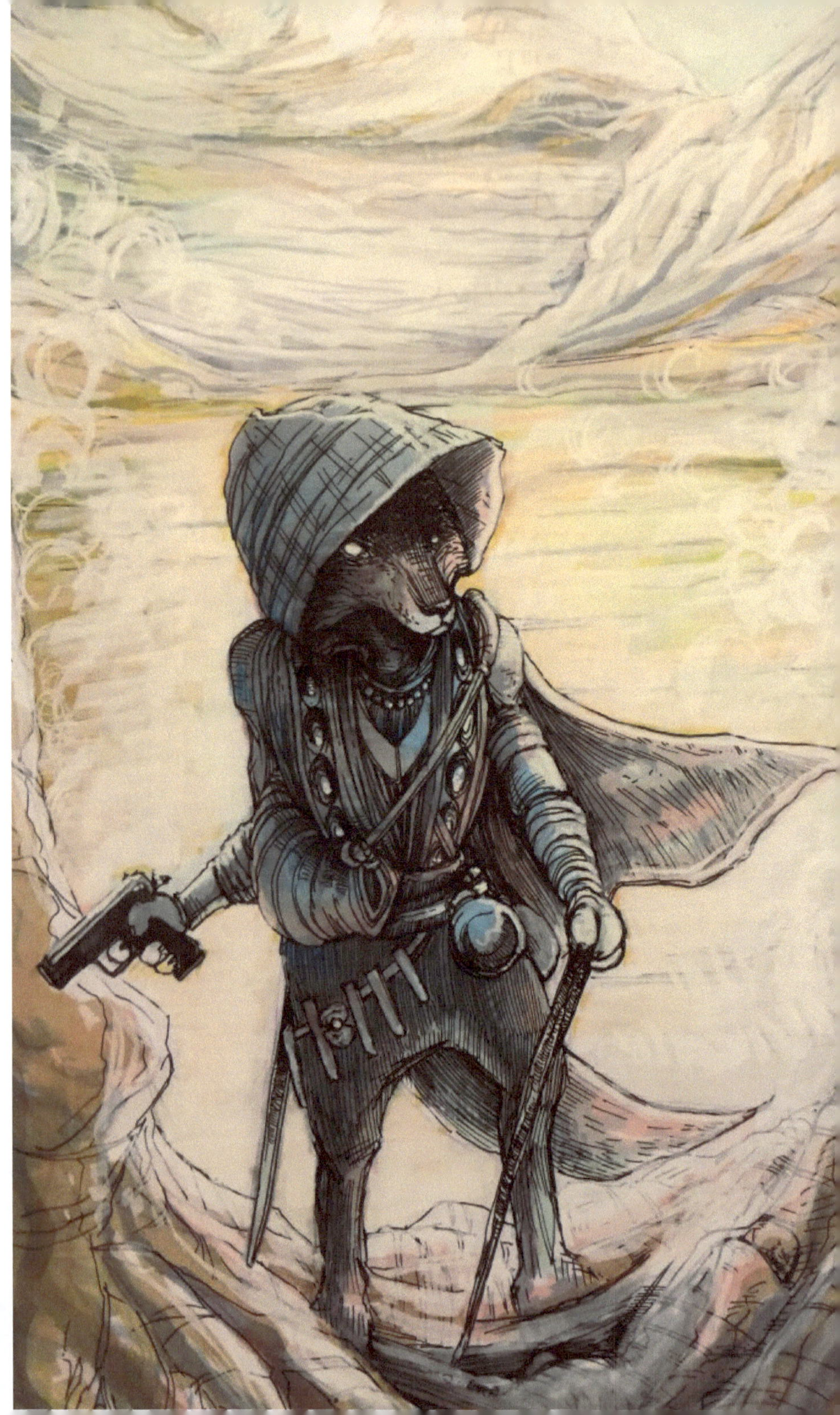

II
1000 years from now

With gun in hand,
He glares out through the toxic air.
The heat clumps around him like a young enemy.

He marches through a summer wasteland.
Shallow footprints disappear in sandstorm breaths.
The air settles on him, weighted down with grit.

His breath is kept.
The wet from throat and eye
Is only for the inside, aligned with only himself.

No voice is heard here.
There is only disaster,
Only loss, only death.

He thinks of his father,
Asks for forgiveness
And looks back at nothing.

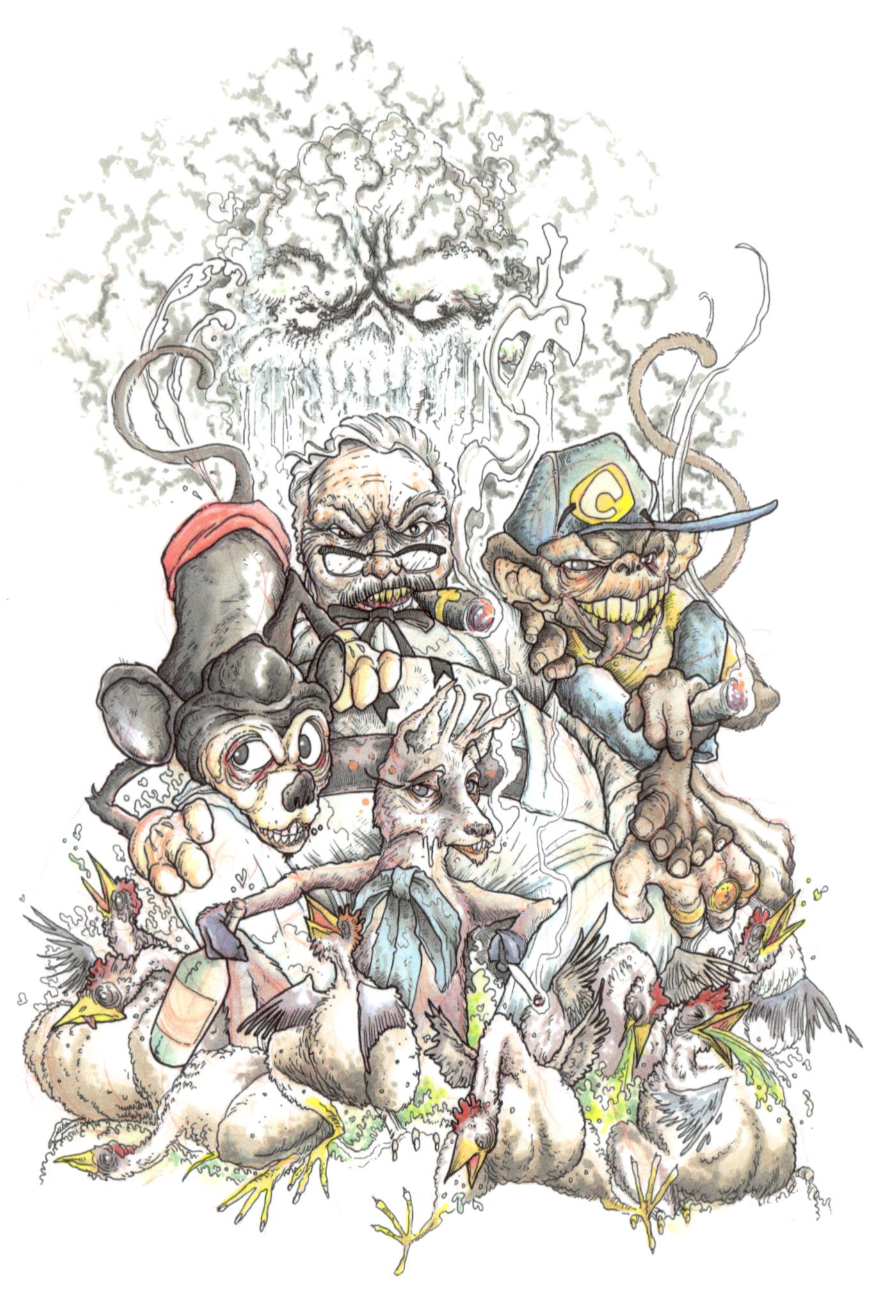

THE WORLD'S NEXT TOP MASCOTS

Mickey's ears droop like
foreskin over his limp head,
hands loaded with toys.

Coco's hat is stitched
onto scalp, wire threaded
through his tail and smile.

Tony's whiskers twitch
as his teeth crack on a spoon
warm and black and bowed.

The Colonel wheelies while
grease runs down his chins, gravy
clogging arteries.

Cool-addled man bubbles
over while brain spikes, craving
a wet, empty rush.

Her fawn hooves flinch,
she bubblies at the mouth, a once dear
baby shammed into remission.

The Captain heaves
in soiled bed, inconsolable,
screaming through the night.

www.linktr.ee/TheWorldsNextTopMascots

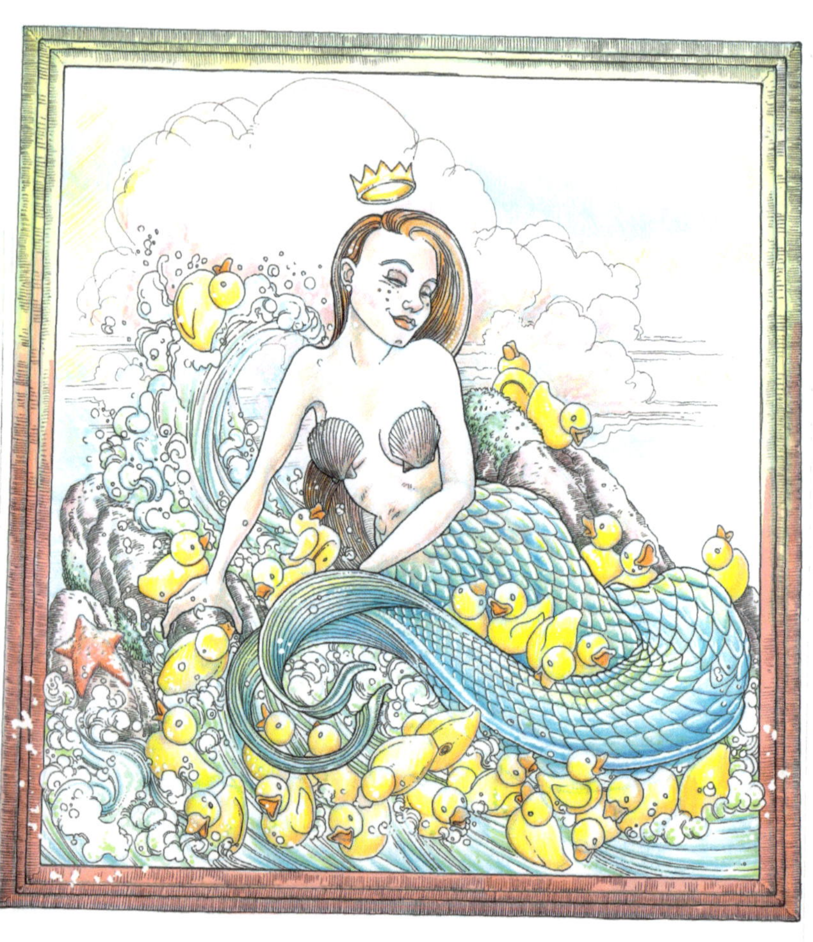

INVASION OF THE RUBBER DUCKIES

We heard the freighter crack
open on the rocks; our lighthouse
had been blinded for days
while the storm had engorged.

At first, we worried about survivors
but the Captain and his single plucky mate
had safely dinghied to 'The Lost Mermaid'
to drown that sunken sorrow.

But their cargo had other ideas.
Buoyant and bright, they bobbed
towards the brown-weeded beach
with yellow flanks and orange bills,

setting the surf a-shimmering
with their shininess. Once ashore,
the plastic mass quacked in hands
and wheezed under feet.

Last year, the oil spill took weeks
to drum. The year before that,
the speedboat's white powder
(mysteriously) disappeared.

But this time, we came skipping,
our children laughing, jostling amongst
the washed-up joy with our thoughts not
on the storm but on the next bath time.

www.linktr.ee/InvasionOfTheRubberDuckies

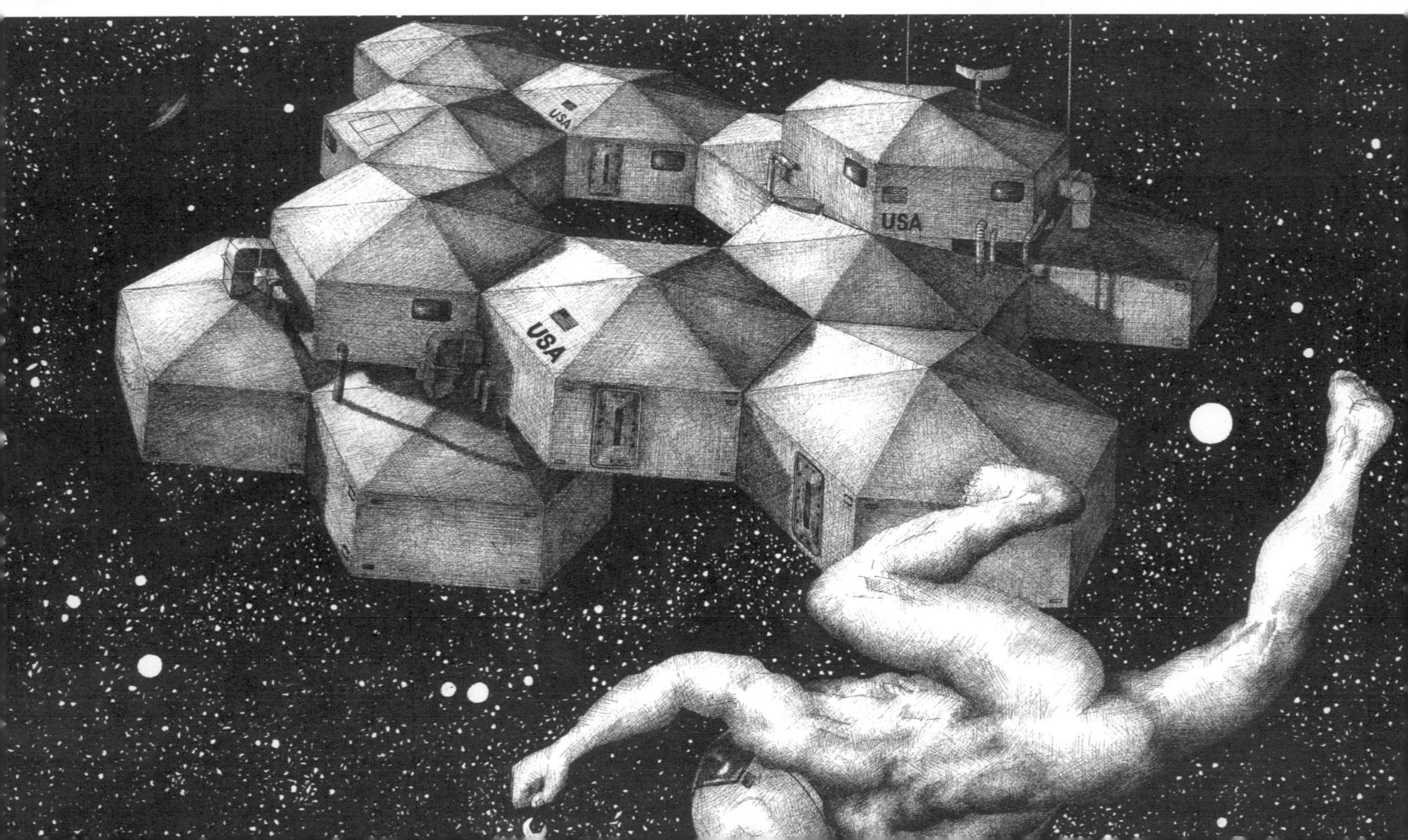
USA
USA
USA

A SPANNER IN THE MECHANICS OF THE SPHERES

art by Bill Shuttleworth

I drew the short fuse and stepped
out and it is moments like this
where you think of whales gulping
from a hole then diving into dark depths
as I take a breath and screw my helmet

on. I have this sticker of an ichthys to the left
of the visor. I believe more in Martians
than in God but I like the way the arcs start
together then curve then play then meet again
but again are drawn away to an emptiness
that once crossed at that liminal point, just like
this station and my body are in motion

now. Now I am the naked fish:
a mammal fish, a flying, floating,
finless, wingless, breathless orbiter,
waiting and praying for something not
to happen. But needs must when there is
something about a loose connection

or an untightened bolt or a red eye
in want of a daisy. I look out and

see we have cast our net so far, past
the moon, the sun, past our belts of rock, built on
the sand of asteroids and meteorites and shooting
stars, way past that planet that isn't a planet any

more. I feel the sweat float away in globes,
interstellar spit that is carried on currents of
solar winds from one quadrant to

another. I am a cog, a spindle, a spoke,
a spaceman in a skin-thin suit and a space that is
blind, like justice, like evolution, like time. This

flare is my last recording.
I hope some rocket will carry this
Major's manmade message home.

www.linktr.ee/ASpannerInTheMechanics

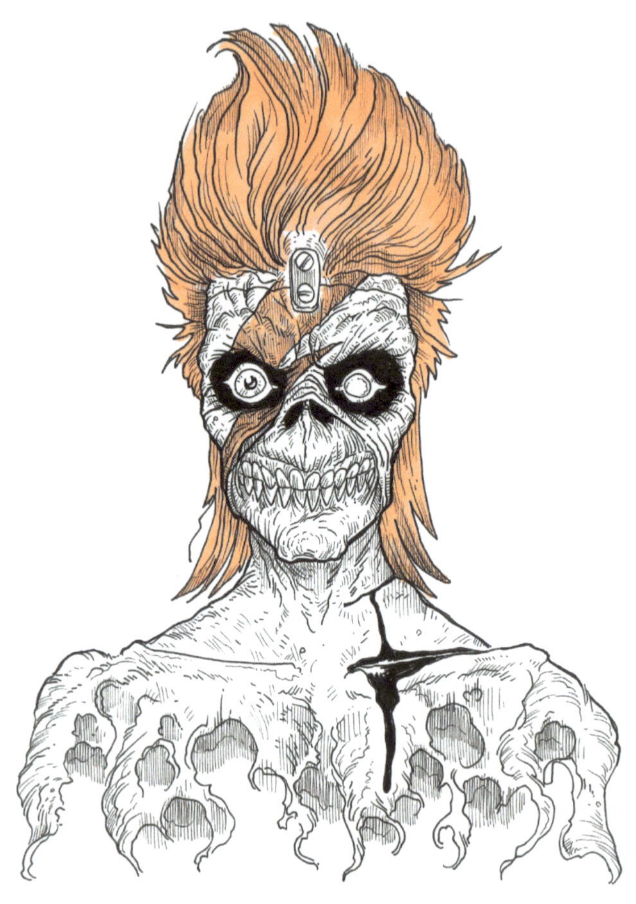

EDDIE STARDUST! LET'S DANCE THE DANCE OF DEATH!

The iron maiden closed on the man who sold the world
and Eddie Stardust was born. Some called him an evil
that men do, wandering through the universe, a starman
lost in the red and the black. In his pockets, infinite dreams
were fashioned. Ashes were laid before him in the shape
of aces. His shoes were made for dancing. When the sky
was clear, you could see this space oddity, this moon child,
this genie of wicker, surrounded by snarling diamond dogs,
beasts branded with a number on their foreheads. Around
all their necks, dog tags glistened, stamped with the motto:
'If eternity should fail, dukes, keep swinging.'
At Christmas, he would dance the width of a circle as if
a ghost navigator ch-ch-ch-changed his life. In a moon
age daydream, the fear of the dark (and of Lady Stardust)
kept him in check. He made the sign of the cross
while playing with madness, perpetually two minutes
to midnight in a golden year, a sweet thing where colours
don't run, sound and vision can be seen running free, and O
you power slave in the foreground of the flight of Icarus,
crashing in the same car as only an iron hero could.
During wasted years of absolute beginners, all those
hallowed troopers became Blood Brothers and young dudes
turned moon children while clairvoyants (now
cracked actors) spent seven years where eagles
dare, loving this alien, quick and dead, rebel and Buddha,
in an empire of the clouds where scary monsters,
ancient mariners, where operatic phantoms, super creeps,
killers all, vow to live under pressure when the wild wind
blows. Even though he couldn't read, a stranger in a strange
land, fame came calling from ground control. And station
to station, Mars to Passchendaele, Eddie Stardust (hallowed
be thy name), this sweet thing, this wrath child, this rock'n'
roll suicide – 'Jump!', we say, 'Jump!' we say, 'Jump,
you man on the edge,' and we will run to the hills,
bowing to no man or maiden.

www.linktr.ee/EddieStardustLetsDanceTheDance

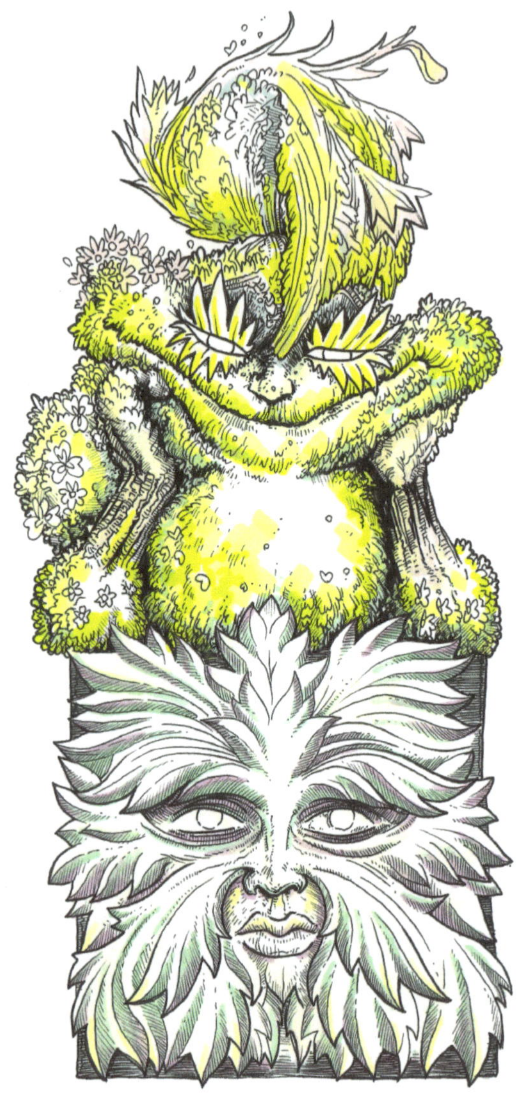

www.linktr.ee/HastingsJackee

HASTINGS JACKEE

Beneath the branches
That twist and sigh,
Where a sea mist creeps
And crazed crows cry,
A leafy whisper,
Emerald sprite freed,
Come see her dance –
Hastings Jackee.

Upon Mayday's dawn,
As the flowers bloom,
The earth cracks wide
And the woods make room.
Jackee emerges,
So fresh and so free,
Born of the soil,
A wild mystery.

From earth she grew,
On bright summer morn,
As the drums beat loud,
A green girl born.
With blossoms in hair,
And roots for feet,
Jackee rises,
A holiday treat.

Through Hastings town,
With the summer's heat,
The sound of laughter,
And tapping feet.
Jackee spins,
As the day turns bright,
A jade-clad guest
In the festival light.

Through the streets she dances,
Beneath sun's gaze,
With ribbons trailing,
In the summer haze.
She sings with joy,
Through fields and lanes,
The season calls,
And she unchains.

When seaside nights
Are warm and sweet,
And the water hums low
With the seeking heat,
She leaps upon the breeze,
With a laugh and a cheer –
Her spirit alive
Now the party is here.

Down crooked streets,
Through market's hum,
Past weathered doors,
And the sound of a drum.
A flicker of green,
Vanished from sight –
Did you see her?
Or was it just light?

Up on the cliffs,
Where the sea birds spy,
The wind pushes past,
And clouds rush by.
She leaps like a gust,
Her footsteps a breeze,
Gone in a heartbeat,
Like wisps in the trees.

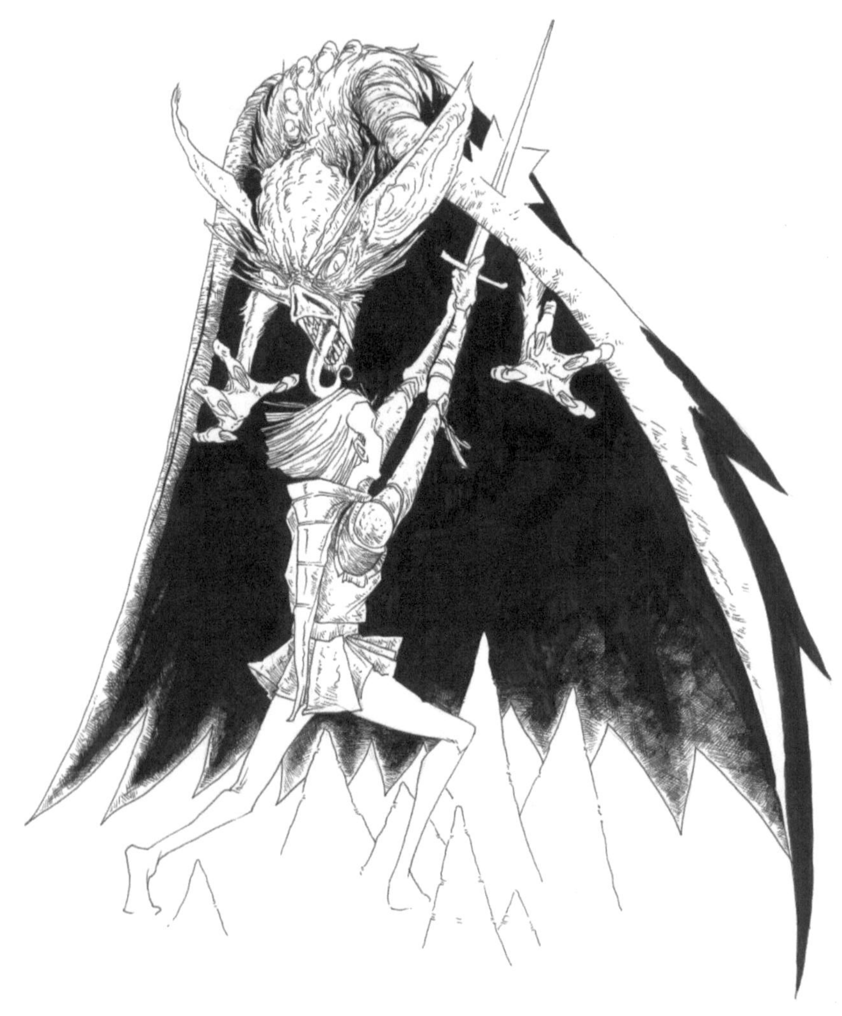

THE PROLOGUE TO THE BALLAD OF SIR ROGER

In which our hero's
strengths, skills and sagas
are lovingly laid out
for all to read

We hear of heroes, honest, brave
Of legends young and old
But one stands tall amongst them all
A gallant knight so bold

He strode through forests bright and wide
Up mountains miles in height
He swam through seas of silver green
Crawled caves both dark and tight

His eyes were piercing, hair so full
His beard was half his fame
With bow so sure and sword so swift
Sir Roger was his name

His cheeks both sparkled, sharp and straight
His nose a spear of gold
With auburn hair whose strands could bear
And lift a mighty load

He knew the knolls like men knew war
He knew the plants like friends
He knew the weather's ebbs and flows
He knew the moles and wrens

Sir Roger rode Ganra his steed
A chestnut-coloured stud
That galloped fierce, fast and firm
With thunderous hoof and thud

The sword that soundly slept by waist
Was sharpened to a fault
It flashed and flailed and fissured air
Like heaven's greatest bolt

Most thought the bottle by his sword
Was liquor, grog, moonshine
But truth be told, it was true dew
Collected time to time

He drank that dew when throat was dry
A pleasure to his lips
Though once he swallowed nectar fine
From loving bees' wing tips

The violin that hung from hip
Was strung by sparrow song
The legacies of its melodies
Played not a moment wrong

Where came his dozen arrows long
A myth has sprung about
The tips were smelt by minotaurs
The shafts, sycamore stout

The feathers fletched from phoenix wings
He tamed that bird in jest
He rode it high through burning sky
Took wisps and left the rest

And so it's sure when songs are sung
Sir Roger's always there
Each verse, each rhyme, each chord,
Each chime rings true through cheery air

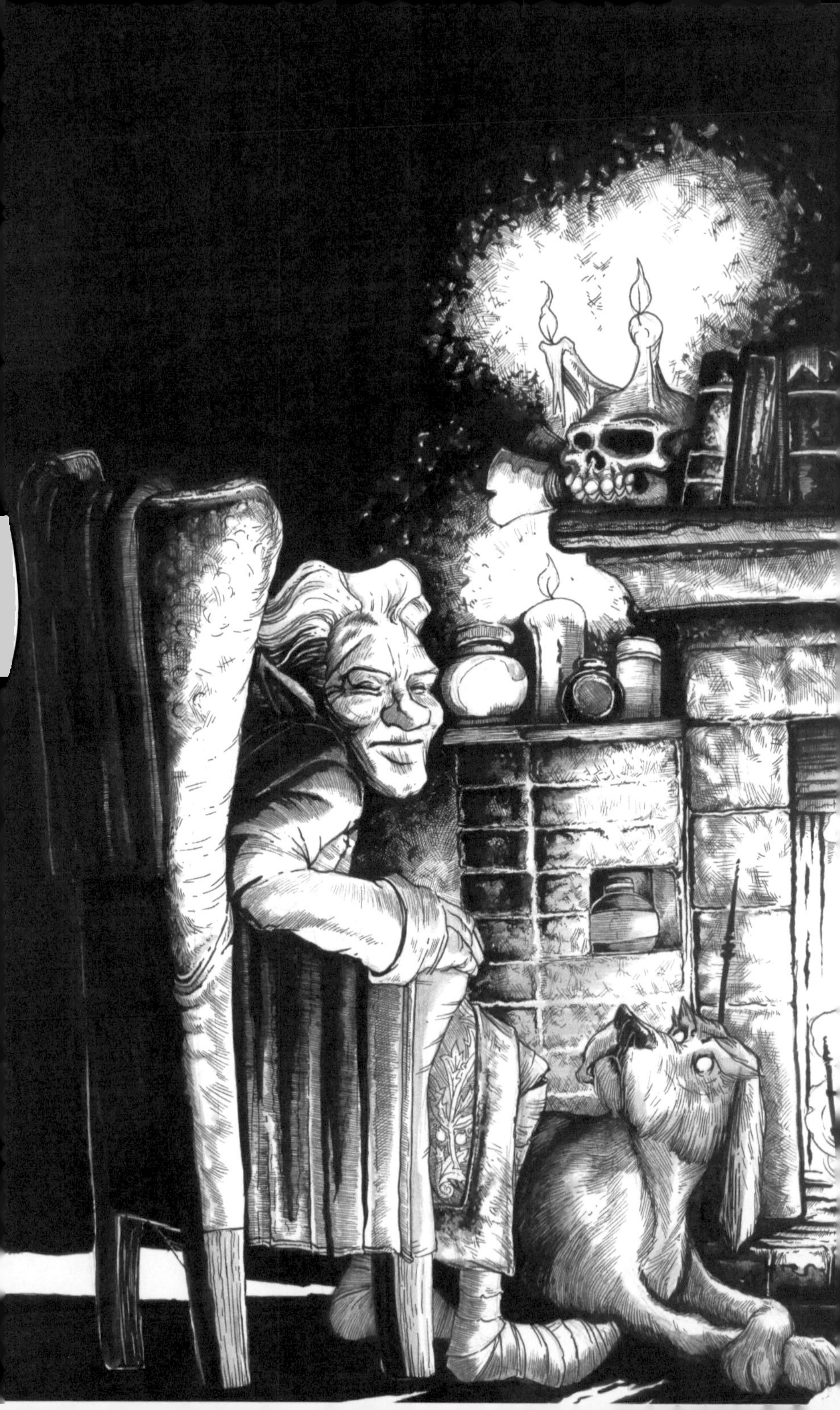

THE BROTHER'S GREED

What follows is the script for Production #29082008 – S01E10 of the Jim Henson series 'The Storyteller', which was presumed forever lost, unfilmed and unread... until now.

FADE IN:

INT. COTTAGE – EVENING

Near to a smouldering fireplace, THE STORYTELLER sits in a tall armchair. At his feet is THE DOG, fearful but alert. THE STORYTELLER turns to the camera and begins to tell a story.

MEDIUM SHOT
LIGHTS TO A WARM GLOW:

THE STORYTELLER

In a hushed-away village nestled between shadowy woods and trundling hills, there lived two brothers – Wilhelm, the eldest, and his little brother, Kerl. Oh, they lived an impoverished life, but were renowned far and wide for their kindness and honesty and generosity, even though they had nothing. They had inherited their father's small farm, but even that came with a price, the house falling apart and the wind attacking it from all sides. And while their land was not fertile, they always managed to scrape by, for they believed that as long as they had each other, they had everything they needed.

THE DOG harrumphs.

THE DOG

I'd rather have a juicy bone...

THE STORYTELLER frowns at the dog and then turns back to the camera.

MIDSHOT

THE STORYTELLER

One evening, as the sun luxuriously sank behind the trees and the wind continued to howl through the branches, battering the house, an old woman knocked at their door. Her back was heavy-hunched, her clothes torny-tattered, and her eyes glinting-gleamed with something ancient and wise. A bit like mine!

THE DOG looks at a broken mirror that leans against the wall. In it, shadows play and dance and the face of the old woman comes into focus. THE STORYTELLER continues, his voice merging with the old woman's.

THE STORYTELLER

"Please," she hesitantly rasped, "I am a poor traveller lost in the woods. May I stay the night and rest by your fire?"

THE DOG shivers.

THE DOG

She gives me the creeps...

THE STORYTELLER smiles a knowing smile.

THE STORYTELLER

Well, not everything is what it seems. Without a moment's hesitation, the brothers of course welcomed her in, offering her the best... well, only seat by the hearth and what little food they had left

— some wrinkly potatoes. As the flames fidgeted in the hearth, the old woman watched them with a knowing smile.

"You have treated me with kindness," she said after eating only half of the meagre portion of potato and licked her lips. "But beware the shadow of greed, for its clasping grip is always closer than you think."

The brothers exchanged quizzical glances but did not ask what she meant. They merely wished her a good night's rest. The next morning, the old woman had vanished, the door locked from the inside. And in her place was a small, blackened key resting on the table. Next to it, there was a note:

THE STORYTELLER reaches into his breast pocket and takes out a piece of paper, yellowed with age and reads it out loud. This time the old women's face appears on the paper, her wrinkles in the folds and creases of the parchment.

THE STORYTELLER

"This key opens a door deep down in a faraway forest, under the tallest, towering oak. Behind the door lies a limitless treasure: but you must be wise, for what you seek is not always what you need."

Wilhelm, the eldest of the brothers, who was always cautious by nature, said "Perhaps we should leave the key where it lies... We have little, but we are content."

But Kerl, who was more adventurous, his eyes turning green in the night light, saw it differently. "What harm could come from searching for the treasure? We could finally live with and not without."

THE DOG drools.

THE DOG

Maybe it's buried bones!

THE STORYTELLER ignores THE DOG and continues.

After much debate and to and froing and arguing and persuading, the younger convinced the older and Wilhelm and Kerl set off in search of the forest. They searched high and low, past glade and vale, through swamp and village, until they found the faraway forest and found the ancient oak, its envious branches burnt at the tips from reaching up, up, up too high, its leaves a dark gold, as if foiled by Midas' hand himself. At its base was a small iron door, so old and rusted and crooked that it seemed to blend into the earth itself. With shuddering hands, Kerl inserted the key, and the door creaked—cracked open.

Inside, the brothers stepped onto a twisting-twirling staircase leading down into the dark, dark, dark below. As they descended further, they found themselves in a vast underground chamber filled with glossy gold, gleaming gems, and radiant riches beyond all measure. And at the centre of the treasure room... sat a simple wooden chest. Of course, Kerl, his eyes wide with excitement, stumbled and rushed to fill his pockets with gold. But Wilhelm, his eyes not reflecting any of the light from the store, was drawn to the plain, wooden chest. It seemed to call to him, as though something important lay within.

"Oh, leave that stupid chest," Kerl snorted, "We have more than enough with these riches!"

But Wilhelm ignored him and could not keep his eyes off the chest. He opened it and found, to his surprise, one single loaf of bread, wrapped in cloth, and a small, dusty bottle of water. At first, he was disappointed, his eyes finally turning to the treasures and Kerl's fastly-filling pockets, but then the old woman's words came back to him like a dream:

"What you seek is not always what you need."

Wilhelm took the bread and water — AND NOTHING ELSE — and closed the chest. As they escaped the groundling chamber, the brothers heard the grinding and gravelling of stone behind them. The iron door had sealed itself shut forever...

At this the cottage door slams itself shut and THE DOG lets out a whimper. THE STORYTELLER rubs THE DOG's ear and continues while sipping from a steaming teacup.

THE STORYTELLER

...and the forest itself seemed to sigh in a warning-relief. Wilheim returned to the ramshackle cottage, but Kerl did not. With all his riches, be bought a tall castle (far from his brother) and surrounded himself with bowing servants and the world's greatest art and glorious treasures all piled high around him, all the fine wines and roast chickens he could gulp down. He had all that he had ever dreamt of... But on the sixth day, he grew ill. No matter how much he ate or drank, he became weaker and weaker day by day. Wilhelm, on the other hand, remained strong and healthy, for he only ate from the loaf of bread and drank the water from the bottle, which magically seemed to replenish itself.

At this THE DOG grunts and snuffles against his empty bowl.

THE DOG

I wish I never ran out of bones.

THE STORYTELLER rummages through his coat pocket while THE DOG looks up expectingly.

THE STORYTELLER

It wasn't long before Kerl realized his folly.

THE STORYTELLER produces an empty hand to THE DOG who collapses to the floor in disappointment. THE STORYTELLER turns back to the camera and continues.

THE STORYTELLER

"I was blinded by greed," Kerl said, his voice hollow and low. "The treasure has cursed me." But brothers are brothers until the end. Wilhelm, upon hearing of Kerl's woes, brought him back home and of course shared his bread and shared his water with his kin. And as the younger brother ate and drunk, his strength returned. They both knew then that the real treasure was not the gold or the gems but the simple magic of the bread and the water, which sustained them in times of need.

THE STORYTELLER searches his other pockets and finds a small bundle of cloth. Camera zooms in as he opens it up to find small bird-like bones with the tiniest amount of meat on them. He drops them into THE DOG's bowl, who snorts with happiness and starts gnawing loudly. THE STORYTELLER turns back to the camera for the last time.

THE STORYTELLER

From that day on, the brothers lived humbly but happily, never wanting more than what they had – and each other – for they understood that true wealth lies not in riches, but in the bonds of brotherhood and in the wisdom to appreciate the simple gifts of life—of knowing the difference between what you want and what you need. And so their tale became a tale for all those that do not know that greed only leads to sorrow, and that true contentment brings true fortune.

HEAD SHOT

THE STORYTELLER turns to THE DOG, leans closer so their noses almost touch.

THE STORYTELLER

Isn't that so?

THE DOG smiles, still chewing on his bones, while THE STORYTELLER turns to the fireplace, warms his hands and contentedly sighs.

SLOW ZOOM OUT TO LONG SHOT

FADE TO BLACK

THE END

www.linktr.ee/TheBrothersGreed

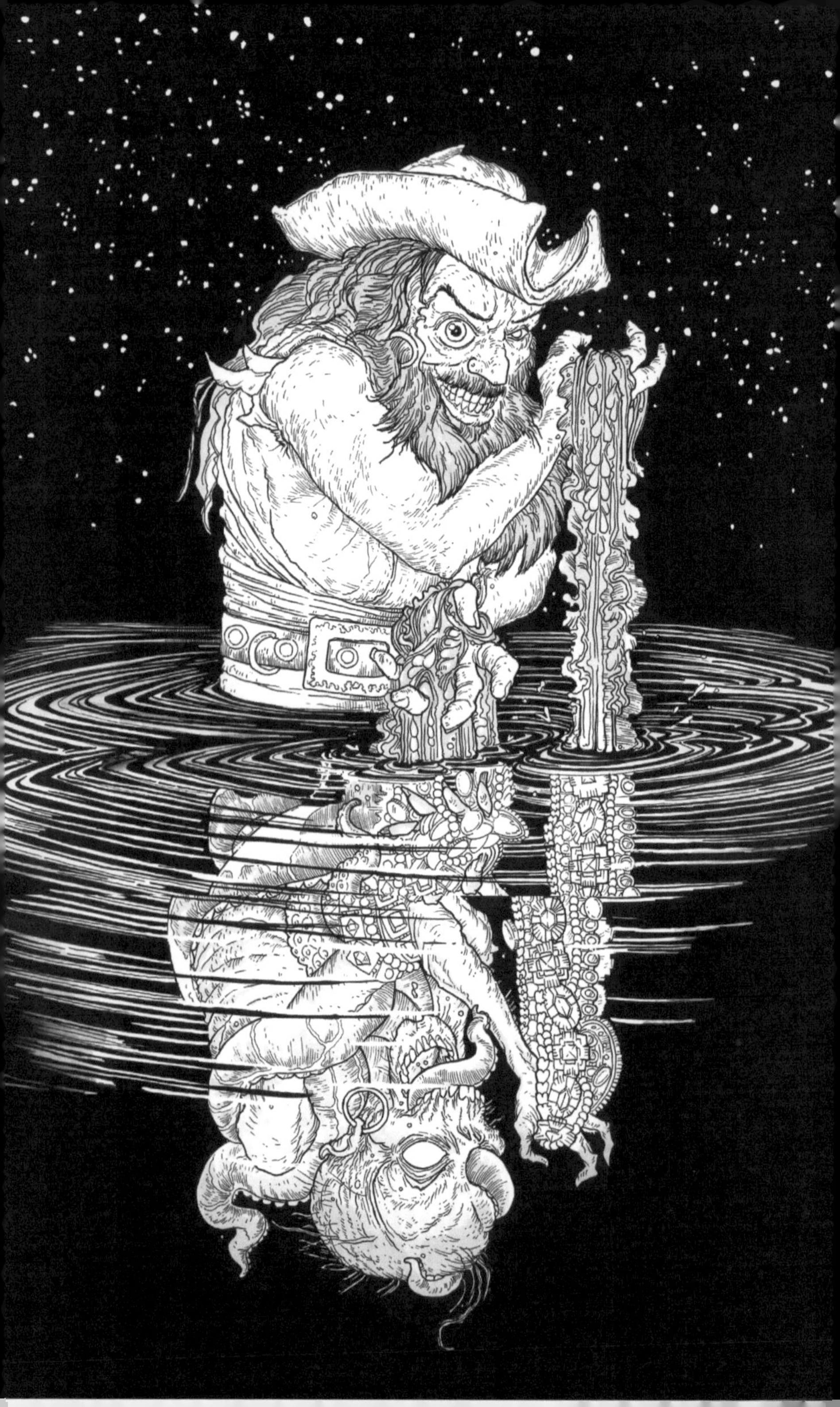

O! DROWN HIM WITH HIS GOLD!

A Sea Shanty

O! Drown Him With His Gold!
O! Drown Him With His Gold!
O! Drown Him With His Gold!
O! Drown Him With His Gold! O!

Through the waves and winds that blow
Here comes a pirate's heart of woe.
He lives and breathes for glint of gold
His dreams all filled with goods untold.

O! Drown Him With His Gold!
O! Drown Him With His Gold!
O! Drown Him With His Gold!
O! Drown Him With His Gold! O!

Looting ships from dusk till dawn,
With cutlass sharp and cannon's scorn.
His crew all cheer as chest soon fills.
He plunders, robs, he raids and kills.

O! Drown Him With His Gold!
O! Drown Him With His Gold!
O! Drown Him With His Gold!
O! Drown Him With His Gold! O!

Fateful night, by cold moon light,
He spies a ship with sail so white.
He charts a course with greedy grin,
But Jones had plans for all this sin.

O! Drown Him With His Gold!
O! Drown Him With His Gold!
O! Drown Him With His Gold!
O! Drown Him With His Gold! O!

A war is waged between the ships
As decks are splintered, sails all rip.
But seas decide which side will win
With crashing wave and raging wind.

O! Drown Him With His Gold!
O! Drown Him With His Gold!
O! Drown Him With His Gold!
O! Drown Him With His Gold! O!

Tempest! Thunder! Darkened sky!
The pirate meets his grim demise.
With gold in hand, he sinks below,
To ocean's deep, a selfish soul.

O! Drown Him With His Gold!
O! Drown Him With His Gold!
O! Drown Him With His Gold!
O! Drown Him With His Gold! O!

Lying low in locker hold,
A tale of greed forever told.
He found his end in Davey's touch.
The pirate craved his gold too much.

O! Drown Him With His Gold!
O! Drown Him With His Gold!
O! Drown Him With His Gold!
O! Drown Him With His Gold! O!

www.linktr.ee/ODrownHimWithHisGold

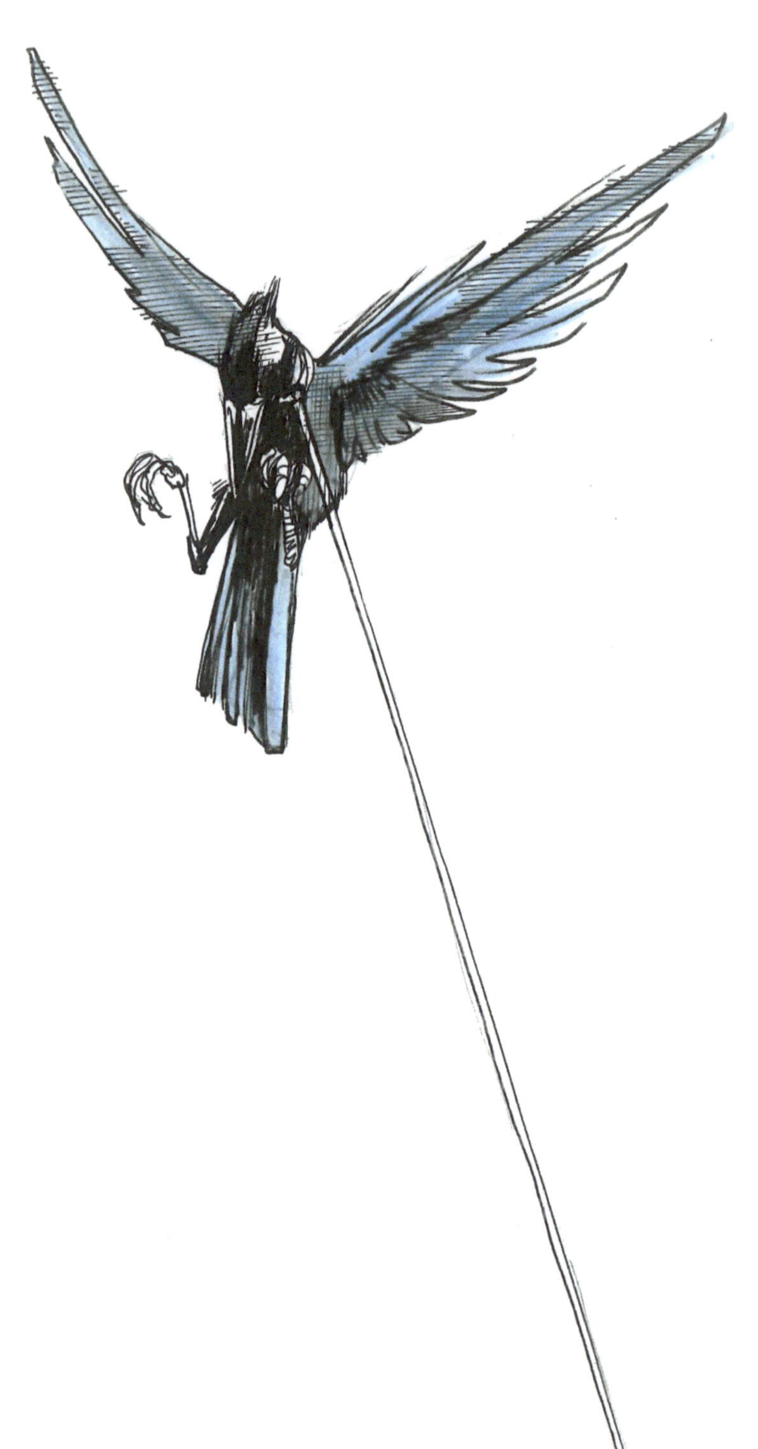

A BIRD ON A STRING

Wild wings whip against the line,
knotted tight in a bind designed.
Strung-up spasm, black and grey,
its feathers catch and strain and fray.

It twists its neck to scan the sky
as claws clutch air too warm, too dry.
It gasps for life not hung mid-flight.
It is wrenched, earthed – a tangled kite.

Narrow shadows of split-end snare
meet tethered hymn and strangled prayer.
The string is taut – it hums and it sings
as clear skies fill with freer wings.

www.linktr.ee/ABirdOnAString

ACKNOWLEDGEMENTS

Luigi:
My parents, Leonardo and Giovannina, for all the sacrifices they made to give me and my brother the best chances in life. My in-laws Dennis and Denise for all their loving support over the many years. My poetry brothers-in-arms Swithun Cooper and Michael Mckimm. Thanks to those that specifically contributed to various aspects of the collection with their time, talent and friendship: Isolde TF Chin, Emeka Diamond, Kyla Gabka, Darren Gash, Kit Griffiths, Will Harris, Erica Hesketh, Gayathiri Kamalakanthan, Vanessa Kisuule, Christy Ku, Charmaine Low, Sara Masry, Lester Gómez Medina, Pẹ̀lúmi Obasaju, Evie Prichard, Mat Rees, A.C. Smith, Leonor Tinajero, Annina Zheng-Hardy.

Mark:
Tessa Wren and Billie-Jean, always have and always been.

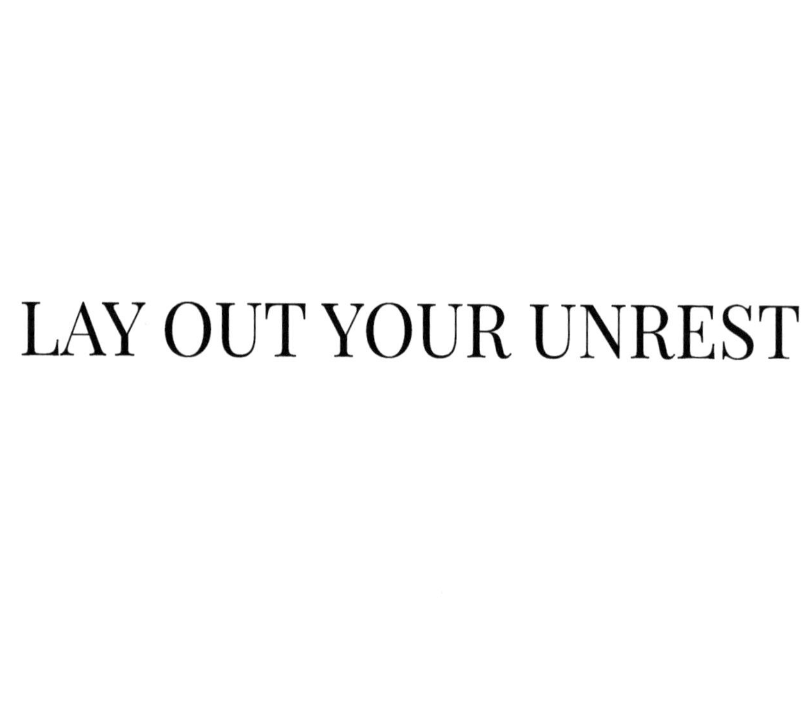

LAY OUT YOUR UNREST

www.ingramcontent.com/pod-product-compliance
Lightning Source LLC
LaVergne TN
LVHW052305100826
845147LV00006B/682